Studies in

Comparative Literature, Translation

and Beyond

Studies in
Comparative Literature, Translation
and Beyond

Parvati G. Aital

Prestige Books International
New Delhi

Published by
Prestige Books International
New Delhi 110 058
Email: prestigebooks@gmail.com
Phone: 9818755529

Associate Office
P.O. Box 2250, Sydney 2001

ISBN: 978-93-82186-86-1

Printed in India

Contents

Author's Note

It is with immense pleasure and a sense of gratification that I am placing before you this collection of essays, which I believe has great academic importance. Contemporary Indian writing in English is rich with its ever-new diversities. It continues renewing itself with the old constructions linguistically and imaginatively. The postmodern thought in all languages begins with the problematization of the nature of the representation of the categories of truth and history. Though some eminent fiction writers have tried to reframe the modernist verbal structure by materializing truth and history in their own way, the academics seek to do the same through a fine amalgamation of research work and reorientation of their individual thinking. Presentation of their thoughts and ideas followed by intellectual discussion is invariably done at seminars and conferences at various levels, and it has become an inseparable part of the intellectual world today.

With my knowledge of five languages, and my keen interest in the translation area, I have translated more than 30 works from English, Malayalam, Hindi and Tulu into Kannada and vice versa. My experience of working in these languages has enabled me to present my papers in a number of state and national level seminars on different occasions. Some of those papers are included in this anthology.

It is imperative for a translator to be a good critic too. Reading literary works from a critical point of view has made me write book reviews too. I have published a number of book reviews in journals and periodicals. I am including some of them in this anthology.

On the occasion of the publication of this anthology, I must express my heartfelt gratitude to all those who have helped me in different ways. First of all, let me thank the Managing Director of Prestige Books International, who has kindly come forward to bring my book to light with great care and concern. I must thank my dear colleague T.K. Ravindran of Bantwal for making suitable suggestions for the book. With great pleasure I share my happiness with my husband Gangadhara Aital.

Kundapura **Parvati G. Aital**

Comparative Literature in the Indian Multilingual Context

Comparative literature has gained a lot of importance in all universities today as an independent branch of study, teaching and research. It was Matthew Arnold who used the expression 'Comparative Literature' for the first time in 1848. Its main objective is to study the literary works produced in different languages, putting them together side by side, and identifying the similarities and differences present in them. Literature and comparative literature are, in fact, two sides of the same coin, and they always influence each other. The different forms of literature like national literature, world literature and general literature are necessary for streamlining the subjects of comparative literature. National literature forms the foundation of comparative literary order. A vast knowledge of national literature is necessary for the study of comparative literature.

The aim of comparative literature is not just the comparison of two works of art by ascertaining their similarities and differences, but the broadening of their perspective through a combination of cultural leniency and literary distinctiveness, and establishing a mutual relation between literary and other human activities.

Practically, comparative literature is different from the study of any single form of literature because it investigates more than one form of it. Therefore, here our outlook should be broader and perspective wider. This is true with regard to other branches of comparative studies like comparative religion, comparative mythology, comparative philosophy, comparative linguistics and so on. The one who pursues his studies in these areas will have to stretch his eyes farther and wider from his own region or nation to the end of the world. In other words, in comparative literature, the frontiers are intentionally crossed with a view to understanding human life in its entirety.

The eminent German poet and philosopher Friedrich Schlegel had spoken about 'The Universal Poetic Art' in 1868. Twenty-five years later Goethe spoke about World Literature. The intention of both of them was to say that literature represented through the works of the best poets in the world was broadly inclusive of all human experiences. Comparative literature tries to reach and understand the frontiers of the same human experience and artistic excellence. One has to understand and appreciate all available literatures in order to succeed in this attempt. Because, this sort of an attempt, like the writing of history, should be able to impart the knowledge of literary revolutions, age and influence, social, political and philosophical environment along with the mutual relations among literatures.

In literary works we normally observe similarities in style, imagery and intellectual thinking. In all of them, some rules and methods are taken to be similar, and they are perfectly followed by all works. From the historical point of view, a common thread binds all of them together. Often they get their inspiration from the same ideals, and therefore they are copies of the same prototype. For example, we may study Ashwaghosh and Kalidas separately. But, if we study them together in the context of the age in which they lived, we have to think of some significant matters like Ashwaghosh's theme of sacrifice, Kalidas' emphasis on Karma, Ashwaghosh's Buddhist and Kalidas' Brahminical line of thought. In order to get a closer view of this, we should study the historical background of the age of the Kushanas and the Guptas. These two authors are the followers of two different religions, but both of them are indebted to Valmiki alike. There is such a decisive similarity among Valmiki, Ashwaghosh and Kalidas from the point of view of thought, expression and technique, that we can make a comparative study of all three of them successfully. In the *Meghdoot* of Kalidas we get the example of a number of poets receiving inspiration from the same source. If we understand the artistic excellence of *Meghdoot* we may easily become familiar with other *Dootkavyas.* These internal similarities make it evident how much Kalidas had been influenced by Valmiki when he composed his poetry.

It is possible to throw light on the various influences leading to the making of a writer through the historical investigation of any literature. This type of study shows that the influence could be hereditary because, creative writing also is equal to the creation of the parts of the human body. And its growth also takes place in the same manner. Life blooms and blossoms, imbibing several things from its surroundings. A literary work also grows in the same way. When we undertake a comparative study we look for similarities. In the light of what we find, when we criticize the text, we, in fact, are trying to find the source of the work in a scientific manner. There is a saying in Sanskrit to the effect that the poets grasp things from others, but they are not thieves: *Naasthiachaurahakavijanaha.* Knowingly or unknowingly they take whatever they find congenial. We have a system of studying famous texts or literary works paying attention only to their language and figures of speech. The drawback of this system is that insignificant theories are given undue importance in it which do not go outside the poet's experience at all. That is why comparative study has been considered the best method, as it gives a deeper insight into it.

The study of comparative literature may include the application of common art patterns, awareness of different literary movements, the trends of the age, the investigation of the subjects discussed in different literatures, their style, structural methodology, analysis of patterns and so on. Extra emphasis may be put on literary relations too.

A question may be raised here about the basis of comparative literature. The literature to be surveyed here is very vast because we have to include in it the entire ancient and modern literature written in different languages. The old methods of criticism have been found to be insufficient today. Modern criticism is not a mere analysis of meaning and textual interpretation. It gives importance to symbols, the investigation of *Rasas* and figures of speeches, analysis of the structural bond, regional features and discrepancies of style. The absence of the vast historical perspective is the characteristic of comparative literature today. However, the traditional methods mentioned above could be enriched through the modern ideas of review on which foundation comparative literature could be effectively placed.

Comparative literature includes comparative review also. Literary review is an attempt to get into the artistic excellence and the excellence of *Rasas* of any literary work. In the context of Indian literature, the lighthouses of literary criticism are Bharata, Dandi, Anandavardhana, Kuntaka and Abhinavagupta. Of course, investigation has been made on poetics in other works too. But in the field only these great writers are called real masters. Abhinavagupta gave it a spiritual touch. In the light of his thoughts only, the Sanskrit and Prakrit literatures were examined and reviewed. And, in the modern Indian languages also literature is mainly read and appreciated in the same manner. The concepts of *Rasa* and generalization have entered the modern criticism through this only. The new and valuable concepts of western literature have enriched it and made it earn a new merit. Perhaps this criticism could be studied along with the criticism of classical literature by Arastu-Horace, and also the modern criticisms of Matthew Arnold, T.S. Eliot and I.A. Richards. It is always good to think about all arts taken together, as it signifies the symbolic expression of any art. In the field of Indian aesthetics, the contributions of Nagendra, Mandhekar and Pantker are worth mentioning here. In Indian comparative literature, the strongest foundation for criticism could only be Sanskrit poetics, enriched by the novel ideas of the west.

When we join these two traditions, we should be aware of two types of dangers—that is, the superfluity of meanings and oversimplification. The biggest danger is empathy; we should see that criticism is rather a vision, not an empathy. What is happening in this field in the west today had happened in India long ago when Abhinavagupta, Bharata, Bhatta, Tauta and Anandavardhana had been severely attacked with the whips of criticism. In fact, literature should be understood and appreciated only through literary relations. The truth is that literature has got its own world. The poets and writers have got freedom to do what they like. In fact, considering literature as the worship of God, they declared that poetry is the source of unique ecstasy. They also said that *shringara* or romance has the most prominent position in poetry. Abhinavagupta took a different philosophical stand and said that *shantaras* or peace is more important. The mutual relation between poetry and philosophy is quite complex by itself, and in the field of literary criticism in comparative study, a broader view is taken in this regard.

In the Indian context, the concept of Indian literature itself is comparative literature, because it suggests more than one literature. The comparative study of Indian literatures has an independent existence of its own. However, unlike the comparative study of French, German or Russian literature, it is not just the scrutiny of fact-based relationship of literary works. The mutual relationship between literatures of two different regional languages of India is not like the relationship between French and German literature, because it is an external relation, and it does not have any spirit in it. They have to establish and develop a relationship till they arrive at a decisive conclusion. India has won in this regard, because it is a multilingual nation. For the study of literatures which grow in this condition, we have to make ourselves familiar with the historical and literary sources of those things which inspire the impulsive and intellectual perceptions within them. The distinctive feature of Indian comparative literature is its difference from that of the west, which makes its independent existence self-evident.

As they are influenced by the same kind of historical and literary sources, there is more scope for study through comparison. It is not a study through some universal perception; it is the study of literatures influenced by historical conditions—just like at the time of the division of our country. Taking the theme of refugees, several novelists have written novels in different languages. The history of Indian literature in different languages is the only field of reference which we can rely upon at present. From this point of view, creating a singular system, the construction of a singular history of Indian literature is essential.

In the present context, on the one hand, Indian literature seems to have been influenced by western literature and, on the other, the people's attention has been drawn towards the recasting of ancient Indian literature in a new light. In the context of Indian comparative literature, the discretion of this influence, as Dr. Amiya Dev says, will not work as successfully as it has done in the case of western comparative literature. Since ours is a third world country, because of our colonial mentality, the English way of thinking has become deep rooted in us long ago. Therefore, when we think about the contextual facts of influence, we should be familiar with the mentality of the writers who have not used that influence as a whetstone to sharpen their talents. Moreover, in the study of this influence, one has to consider the anxiety which the Indian writers lived with. On the one hand, there was the writer who grew with the uninterrupted flow of Sanskrit literature, and on the other, there was the pull towards English literature. The historical interpretation of this ambiguous position is essential for writing the history of Indian literature, and it is desirable that an analysis of the anxiety caused by the conflict between the Western influence and our traditional literature be made.

When a work of art in one Indian language is studied, it is essential to concentrate on the personality of the author, the age and the environment, and the cause-effect relations in the case of racial studies. But in the study of comparative literature, we should know the deeper forms of cause-effect relationships. That is why, the writing of the history of comparative literature, different from the history of literature, becomes possible only through the techniques of comparative literature. For example, the Bangla poet Madhusudan Dutt, at first, started writing in English. The history of literature just gives a hint to this. But comparative literature tells you the reason for it, and also explains why some of the writers in those days, liked to write in English. The history of literature tells us when Mr. Dutt started writing in Bengali, but comparative literature finds the reason for it and talks at length about it. In fact, when we think on the basis of the elements of solidarity, a singular conception of comparative study of Indian literature is possible. In writing the history of comparative literature, the relation between Western literature and Indian literature is different from the mutual relationships among the Indian literatures in various vernacular languages. The former will certainly be historical, and the latter partly historical and partly aesthetic. Since the third world has come into existence, much difference has not come in its historical relation with western literature.

It is evident that for Indian comparative literature, different from that of the west, the concept of a literary history is significant by itself. Being a multilingual nation, the building of this concept is possible only from the comparative ground. The concept of Indian literary history on a singular basis, in a singular form, could be built, using the techniques of comparative literature. The history of Indian literature means Vedic Sanskrit, Pali, Prakrit and so on, along with Urdu and other literatures. Indian writings in English also are included in this. At present, from the comparative as well as critical ground, the study of comparative regional literatures is going on. But the evolution of a singular Indian literature has not been possible from the utilitarian perspective. According to Sujit Mukherjee, in this type of study, more emphasis is given to a detailed study of history rather than literature. In the initial stage, the orientalists of the west restricted themselves to the historical study of Vedic or Sanskrit literature of the Middle Ages. The works of Albrecht Weber, Winternitz, Edwin Arnold, R.W. Frazer and so on could be cited here. In the investigation of ancient literature too, the attitude of these scholars remained analytical instead of being critical. In the context of Max Mueller's book *The History of Ancient Sanskrit Literature*, R.K. Dasgupta says that most of the European historians have propagated an archaeological view towards ancient Indian literature, instead of showing critical response. These scholars, later when they turned their attention to the writing of modern Indian literary history, narrowed their views to linguistics, grammar and diction, and were indifferent to the analysis of literature. Thus till the end of the 19th century, the meaning of the history of Indian literature was only literature produced in ancient Sanskrit, Pali and Prakrit. In the beginning of the 20th century, when the attention of the scholars was turned to the writing of literary history of Indian languages, it was believed that the history of Indian literature was the sum total of the history of literatures produced in all regional languages. They were written following the model of different histories of English literature. However, such a method was not suitable to be adopted in a multilingual nation like India.

In the present context, it is possible to consider that the literature of one region could be written in any language. Multilingualism is the distinctive feature of this nation. Because of this, two problems arise before us. 1) As a result of having different languages, the direct knowledge of the entire Indian literature is impossible for a single historian, and therefore it cannot be written on a general historical frame. Moreover, for a comprehensive literature like this, we do not have a model, accepted by all. 2) The lack of any critical perspective which could be used to evaluate the literatures produced in different languages, which in turn would smoothen the work of writing of Indian literary history. However, the reason for this lack is nothing but its inability to have a holistic view of Indian literature. The biggest weakness of the Indian writers is that they compare their works with those of the westerners. It hinders the growth of the critical outlook. Besides, by restricting the history of literature to any one literature, or, not turning their attention to the study of mutual relationship of regional literatures, the writing of literary history has become the literary history of only one language, and so, the comparative system has denied assistance to the critical view.

In order to be free from these two problems the writing of the history of Indian literature should be based on the elements of solidarity. Also, one has to take the assistance of critical perspective which is there in the comparative system. The Indian linguistic environment introduces us to the vast expanse of regional languages, literatures, actions and reactions of various literary cultures. That is why, in the writing of its history, a broad frame of reference should be set. The history of literature should be written from the intellectual ground rather than the linguistic, social or cultural side of the system of life. Therefore literature should not be misinterpreted as mere literary manifestation, but the production of literary tradition through framed units other than language.

Among the Indian scholars, Aurobindo was the first to try and succeed in building the concept of Indian literature on the frame of reference to the elements of solidarity in his book *Indian Literature*. He identified the central voice, form and aesthetic value of Indian literature from the Vedic Age to the *Bhakti* Age and accepted them as the expression of Indian cultural mind. According to Aurobindo, the original voice of Indian mind has spiritual insight in its psyche. After him, Nagendra, Suneetikumar Chatterjee and Krishna Kripalani also referred to the elements of solidarity, accepting the same central voice through which the integrity of Indian literature could be identified. Krishna Kripalani said that in spite of the changing forms of Indian literature in different languages at different times, some principles have proved themselves to be more unique than others, which never get destroyed by time. One of them was a strong perception of unlimited goodness. This sense has become one with the pageant of Indian literature just like the Himalayas filled with ice-bergs. Perhaps the framework of a singular Indian literature may get ready with the help of these principles of unity.

In the construction of the history of Indian literature, similar kind of information and knowledge could be taken from literatures of different languages. Here, attention should be paid to the principles of not only unity, but also diversity. Because, while admitting that the Indian tradition based on solidarity is unbroken, the fact cannot be ignored that the individuality of our writers writing in different languages is also significant. For example, the epic tradition has greatly influenced all our writers, and there are a lot of similarities in the poetry of Tulsidas, Kamban, Kriibas, Mukteshwar, Pampa and Kumaravyas. But their diversities also are interesting to study. In spite of coming from the same tradition, they are different from each other in a queer way.

The study of similar types of Indian streams is essential for the construction of the concept of Indian literary history. The origins of these streams are the ancient Vedic and Sanskrit literature, followed by myths and legends, religious scriptures, the *Ramayana*, the *Mahabharata*, art, music, folklore and so on. The reactions of the Indian writers to the influence of Arab, Parsi, and Western literature also should be studied. Here, for connecting other subjects like the study of social, political and economic conditions with the study of literature, one has to rely on social sciences. The commonly agreed upon fact is that any literary work is the specific production of a specific Time and Space. And therefore, the study of every suitable unit which influences the human deeds becomes imperative. That is why the study of all contemporary social and political institutions, thoughts and beliefs, laws and values becomes necessary in the writing of Indian literary history, as it regulates the life stream of any country. Thus by studying the Indian literature produced in different languages in the context of motifs, myths, images, symbols, structure, tone and theme, it is possible to identify the patterns of literary actions, based on which, an all Indian frame of reference could be built and the construction of the concept of Indian literature made possible.

For the writing of a singular literary history of Indian literature, we have to take the help of comparative literature. Comparative criticism is the pillar on which it stands, and in its absence the critical analysis of the poetics of Indian literature is impossible. Today, the instrument of western criticism is being used more than the instrument of Indian poetics. However, for the traditional and modern form of Indian literature, any one method of criticism is of no use. For that we have to create a new literary criticism or poetics. Because of the tradition of Indian poetics joining hands with the western tradition, our standard of critical analysis has come down. Several Indian scholars have proved the relevance of Indian poetics in the context of modern literature through a comparative study of the criticism of Indian and western theories. Indeed the Indian poetics will enlighten the foreign research work, giving it a new meaning. On the other hand, the fields in which the Indian criticism looks experimental, only through the comparative scrutiny of western poetics, a profitable and useful construction of an all-Indian critical methodology, and the analysis of various dimensions of a singular history of Indian literature becomes possible. But, for this type of analysis, the critical methodology should be interdisciplinary in nature.

The analytical system of literary history is double-faced in itself. On the one hand, there is the study of the literariness of the history of literature, and, on the other, the more relevant meta-critical study. With this kind of study only, it is possible to identify a common quality in different literatures, and the conception of a singular Indian literature is possible.

In the 19th century the concept of world literature had been limited to the literature produced only in Europe. The European tradition had been moulded by its own culture along with Semitic culture, and it evolved slowly and steadily with the passing of time. That is why the literature of South-West Asia, which is found in the Bible, is considered a part of world literature. It was at the same time that comparative literature also developed in Europe. In fact, what was accepted as comparative literature was the study of a literary genre, criticism and theory and literary movements of two or three writers and their works in different European languages. Goethe's interpretation of world literature also was the same. Thus, till the beginning of the 20th century, comparative literature remained within the limits of European literature. However, in the 20th century there was a revolutionary change in the meaning of world literature. Its Eurocentric concept crossed its limit and was spread all over the world, entering even other fields of life. Today world literature is being studied on a universal level. In the books on world literature, separate chapters have been devoted to the literatures of different nations.

In the Indian context, Rabindranath Tagore had used the expression 'World Literature' for the first time in 1907. In one of his speeches he said that if we are to understand a man who expresses himself through his deeds, inspirations and aspirations, we should make ourselves familiar with the medium of entire human history. Man forever works for the fulfillment of his aims and tries to develop meaningful relationships with the others around him. Man wants to see an immortal and universal man in history rather than a common, local man. He gives expression to his soul's joy through the medium of words in world literature. That man may be described as having an unhealthy look, he may be a stoic or an epicurean, but the spirit within him is always the same. Tagore makes it clear that just like this world is not the sum total of all the pieces of this earth, literature also is not just a collection of the writers of the whole world writing in different languages. Therefore we should rid ourselves of the narrow-mindedness of nationalism. We should see each and every work of art from the point of view of its singularity, and identifying this singularity is possible only through world literature. Thus we do not find any difference between world literature and comparative literature. According to Tagore, we have to study comparative literature admitting the fact that the literature produced in different languages of the world is one whole unit, because, world literature in which innumerable historical and internal spiritual relationships are evolved, the discovery and study of these things itself is the work of comparative literature. It is true that the difference between the two is clear with regard to the comparative system, but the more we try to define this difference, the wider the field of study becomes. The field of world literature overlaps with the field of comparative literature.

Works Cited

Arnold, Edwin. *Indian Poetry*. New York: Hurst, 1884.

Arnold, Matthew. *Letters of Matthew Arnold*. London, Macmillan, 1895.

Aurobindo. *The Foundation of Indian Culture*. Vol. IV, Pondicherry.

Chatterjee, Sunitikumar. *Languages and Literatures of Modern India*. Calcutta: Bengali Publishers, 1963.

Dev, Amiya. "Comparative Indian Literature." Paper presented at a Seminar at Guru Nanak Dev University, Amritsar, 1981.

Frazer, R.W. *A Literary History of India*. London: The Bookman, 1920.

Kripalani, Krishna. *Modern Indian Literature.* Bombay: Nirmala Standard Publishers, 1968.

Nagendra. *Bharateeya Vagmaya.* New Delhi: Indian Literature, 1958.

Remak, Henry H.H. *Comparative Literature, its Definition and Function.* Penn State University Press, 1966.

Schlegel, Friedrich. *Universal Poetic Art.* 1868.

Sycee, R.A. *Year Book of Comparative and General Literature.* 1966.

Weinstein, Ulrich. *Comparative Literature and Literary Theory.* Bloomington: Indiana U.P. 1973.

New Woman in the Early Indian Fiction

The Indian novel, in its present form, has its roots in the west. In India, of course, there were other narrative forms like epics and legends in Sanskrit and romances and ballads in regional languages. But they are entirely different from what we call novel today. Ancient India had a 'non-linear, cyclical and chronologically diversified narrative, which was in contrast with the linear, chronologically streamlined single voice narrative' which appeared in the west after the Renaissance. Besides, there was the oral narrative tradition. However, it regained its importance during the national freedom struggle and became popular only with the illiterates.

English education at schools gave scope to books written on the western model. Consequently, it created a readership which was not interested in the traditional Indian narratology. These readers developed a liking for the books written by the English writers. Several English books were translated into Indian languages, and these had a tremendous influence on the young readers. These translations became a model for the Indian writers to explore new narrative models. Towards the end of the 19th century, the novel developed in India as a prose narrative. It carried on the theme of man-woman relationship which had already been there in the traditional narratology. Added to it, the socio-political concerns of gender were also brought into it. The multiplicity of the forces which focused on the women issues and the presence in the form of the forces which constructed woman as a participant in the nationalistic discourse, brought in several psychological issues to bear upon it—issues that were more political than personal.

Modernity holds a very conspicuous place in the history of any society in any age. When we trace the history of the popularity of the concept of modernity, we may see the term being used with respect to the European initiatives towards the overhauling of the socio-cultural and intellectual scenario in the third world countries. If we extend this notion of modernity to colonialism, we get the expression 'colonial modernity.' Later on, it became a discourse with a strong undercurrent of power, and gave immense scope for gender reading too. Gender was an endemic issue for modernity in Victorian England. A look into the construction of womanhood in the Victorian England shows us the way how it gave rise to the New Indian womanhood. It was during this period that the British society assigned separate spheres demarcated as the private and public for women and men respectively. Girls were trained from their childhood days to consider the domestic space as theirs. That dictated the type of education to be given to them. Modernity brought into effect new notions about femininity which were centered on the identities attributed to woman, based on her biological body—that of a wife and a mother.

The emergence of novel as a new genre in all regional languages coincided with the incorporation of the corresponding societies into the Victorian project of modernity. Towards the end of the 19th century, colonialism in India had become very powerful and influential. The response of the Indians to colonialism was quite complex and mixed. On the one hand, they had developed a liking for English education which, they thought, was a sign of modernity. On the other, they loved their nation, and hated the cruelty of the colonial rulers. The strong sense of nationalism made them uphold the native traditions and glorify the heritage of India. At this time, great Indian leaders like Raja Ram Mohun Roy, Dayananda Saraswati, Ishwar-chandra Vidyasagar, Gopalakrishna Gokhale and others dedicated themselves to Reformist activities in the country. Their social organizations like

Arya Samaj and Brahmo Samaj swept through the country, bringing tremendous changes in all spheres of Indian life at a breath-taking pace. The exploitation of women and the atrocities on them were the major questions taken up by these Reformists. Naturally, they had their space in literature too. The early novel in almost every Indian language was woman-centered, and situations were created that they were left to themselves, act independently and take their own decisions.

Many cultural traditions in India ran parallel to each other towards the end of the 19th century. The Renaissance in Bengal took up the nationalistic discourse as its theme. The Urdu tradition negotiated with the institution of courtesan, cross-race gender relations and the support of the Mughal court which was weakening. The Punjab tradition emerged after its fight with the Anglo-Sikh wars and its getting colonized. The Maharashtrian consciousness questioned all power structures including those of religion, caste and gender. In Kerala, it was the revolt against the exciting social conventions like the exploitation of women in Nair and Namboodiri communities. In Karnataka, it came up with a realization and urge for a social change. Deeply influenced by the pervasive urge for national independence, the Telugu novelist turned his attention towards the social structure, where his conscience impinged upon the prevalent social evils of inequality and iniquity. In Orissa, with the gradual decay of feudal culture, the rising middle class was torn between the two extremes of the rural and the urban, giving the novelists one of their central themes—the rural-urban binary.

A study of the new woman in the early Indian fiction is the objective of this essay. Hence I deem it convenient to discuss the major works of the eminent authors of those times in various regional languages of India—the works in which women issues are seriously discussed.

In Hindi literature, Premchand stands out as the major novelist of the times. Strongly influenced by the reformist movement, he believed that women played a very important role in the development of the society and the nation. He said that the society which looks down upon women would never prosper. His novels glorified the institution of marriage, and insisted that it is essential in the life of an individual for the fullness of one's personality. Particularly, a woman should never be deprived of the opportunity of becoming a mother.

Premchand has never given a positive picture of women speaking against marriage. A character called Malati in his *Godan* decides not to marry and simply lives together with her lover Mr. Mehta. The author disapproves of it, and brings out a change in her life at the end of the novel. Premchand is unhappy about the polluted atmosphere of the system of marriage in India. The women are made victims to the cruel dowry system, early widowhood and mismatched marriages. The freedom of choice had been curbed for girls by their parents who made undue fuss about caste, creed, family lineage, status, horoscope and so on. Many of Premchand's novels deal with these problems of women.

Influenced by the principles of Arya Samaj, Premchand believed that a woman's chastity should be protected at any cost. In his novel *Pratijna* the heroine Prema, when she finds her chastity at risk, fights for protecting it like a she-lion. Suman in *Sevasadan*, even though she becomes a dancing girl and prostitute, is very much conscious of her chastity. In *Karambhoomi*, poor Munni is heart-broken when she is molested and raped by the Whites.

Premchand describes a woman's desperate condition due to a mismatched marriage in *Nirmala*. Because of poverty, her father gives her away in marriage to Totaram, who is as old as her father. Unfortunately, she becomes a victim to his suspicious nature. Life becomes a constant struggle for her and she dies, being unable to put up with the mental torture. In the novel *Rangbhoomi* Indu gets a husband, who never loves her. In

Karambhoomi Naina's fate also is the same. However, both of them constantly oppose the wicked deeds of their husbands and suffer throughout. In *Godan* Khanna's wife Govindi is an educated woman. When her husband neglects her, she comes out of her house. Premchand agrees that these husbands are cruel and inhuman, but he does not approve of women breaking the relation by coming out of the family. The reason for it is his faith in the ancient Indian belief that an ideal woman is the incarnation of forgiveness and sacrifice, selfless service and purity. He gives the picture of an ideal couple in *Godan* through Hari and Dhania. In Premchand's opinion, a woman can take any amount of freedom, but she cannot forget her responsibility of keeping her home. She can revolt or retaliate, but only within the limit of her family.

Premchand is firmly against the society which suspects the character of a woman. If a man gives shelter to a woman in her desperate condition, the people spread scandal about them (*Godan*). He condemns this narrow-mindedness of the society. About prostitution, he says that it is not the fault of a woman, but that of her circumstances. In his novel *Sevasadan*, his views about prostitution have been expressed. Suman becomes a prostitute because of her helpless circumstances. Her father takes bribe and goes to jail. So, she has to marry a very poor man. Her tender beauty and Gajanand's inability due to poverty do not go together. And the result is a mutual suspicion. Suman runs away and becomes a prostitute. Because of this stigma, her younger sister's marriage stands cancelled. The reaction starts from here. The younger sister turns out to be different from Suman. She accepts Sadan as her husband. Gajanand becomes a recluse, and his penance begins from here. Suman also begins to lead a chaste life by establishing Sevasadan for reforming the life of the prostitutes. Suman's character makes the reader feel sympathetic towards her. At first she has a feeling that there is freedom in the life of prostitutes. But later she realizes the pains and agonies suffered by them. Premchand's attempt here is to investigate the new possibilities in the life of the prostitutes.

Among the Bengali novelists, Bankimchandra Chatterjee's name comes first. After receiving English education, he worked under the British government for 33 years as Deputy Collector. His source of inspiration to write novels was his reading of English literature. Since he was well-versed in English language, it was easy for him to write his first novel in English titled *Rajmohan's Wife*. Its theme and plot were almost like that of a detective novel. But the novel gave a very bold picture of a female character called Matangini. That 18 year old girl, though born and brought up in a village, wearing a *ghosha* to cover her face, exhibits a lot of courage and wisdom in making the plot of the dacoits meet with a tragic failure.

In his later novels also, women characters are adorned with rare qualities. But none of them is far from reality. In *Vishvriksha* he discusses the problem of lust—how it destroys the happiness of the married couples. Bankim's views of an ideal married couple could be seen in Shreesha and Kamalamani. Sooryamukhi is another character, affectionate and faithful to her husband Nagendra. But she loses her peace of mind because of Nagendra's lust for Kundanandini. The problem of polygamy also is discussed here.

Rajani is another important novel of Bankimchandra. His growth as a novelist could be seen here in the psychological analysis of the limited number of characters. The heroine Rajani, though blind, is very shrewd, sensitive and intelligent. Her individuality is seen in her standing firm to wait till she achieves her goal of marrying the man she loves. Her well-wisher Lavangalata also is a lovable character. She helps Rajani get the man she loves. She suffers in her personal life, being the young second wife of an old man. But she faces all the difficulties boldly.

Bankimchandra's novel *Indira* addresses the problem of child marriage. Indira, the heroine, gets married as a child. Her departure to her husband's house is delayed under the pretext of the limited earning capacity of her husband, the fact being her father's social pride. Indira's wishes and desire to join her husband and live with him are sandwiched between the confrontations of the two male egos. When finally the longed for journey is undertaken, fate intervenes in the shape of dacoits who snatch all her jewels and clothes away, along with her 'social identity.' But surprisingly, they do not cause any physical harm to her. Retaining her virtue like this may be a technique used by the author from the narrative point of view. All her escorts run away from her, and she wanders alone. Fortunately she finds the house of an old Brahmin who takes her as a servant to cook in his house. Through her expertise and sincerity in her work, she wins the hearts of all. The Brahmin's son Raman and his wife Suhasini try to trace her family and find out her husband Upendra. They invite him to their house, without knowing anything about Indira's past. Besides, Indira has changed her name as Kumudini now. Kumudini behaves at two different levels. Outwardly she behaves like a maid who falls in love with the guest, and elopes with him. At the second level she shows the need to do so because he is her husband, who she fears perhaps would not accept her if he hears her story. The drama continues till at last they are united. Of course, Indira feels unhappy when her husband responds positively to her advances. But she decides to correct him later. Here the author unknowingly projects the male chauvinism by making Indira's husband not feel guilty of falling in love with another woman and eloping with her. But he is full of admiration for the boldness, intelligence and firmness of mind in Indira.

Rabindranath Tagore is another Bengali writer who has given a lot of importance to women issues in his novels. His first successful social novel was *Chokerbali*. It is the story of a young widow Binodini who fails in her love. Being a widow, she is deprived of the right to love, and she does not have any light in her life. During the earlier period of her association with Mahendra she simply tries to tempt him without being sure of what she wants. When in the end she realizes that what she longs for is a man's love, to her shock she finds Bihari at her feet. She feels tired and says to him: 'I shall pray and do penance that I may have you as mine in our next life. In this life I dare not hope for more, I do not deserve it.' Binodini is presented in the novel as 'the eternal feminine, trudging through the ages in quest of her lover—weary with pain, distracted with longing, bursting with the throb of desire, trudging through poetry, through song, until there she stands on the other shore crying 'Ferry me across boatman.'

In the novel *Yogayog*, Tagore depicts the glory and greatness of a very sensitive woman called Kumudini. She is the wife of a rugged, uncouth man called Madhusudan, who treats her cruelly, taking for granted that she is just a piece of his property. But later Kumudini manages to bring about a transformation in him through her skill and will power. At first she looks like a beautiful, ineffectual angel, but later turns out to be a very powerful character with the spiritual armour within her. She walks out of her husband's house just like Nora in Ibsen's *Doll's House.* At this, her husband loses his temper and he develops a contact with a widow. Kumudini hears about this, in spite of which, she returns to the Bear's Garden: 'One hopes that the mother will be even more successful than the wife in humanizing and ultimately spiritualizing the rugged Madhusudan.' (*Rabindranath Tagore: A Critical Introduction*, 85)

Tagore's most ambitious work was the novel by name *Gora.* In this novel he projects the vision of the role of an individual in the renascent India. Krishna Kripalani compares this novel to Tolstoy's *War and Peace*. Gora is the main character in the novel (Gora means White) He is strictly orthodox in all his thoughts and deeds. He hates the principles of Brahmo Samaj. But, by nature he is very good, staying miles away from evils, falsehood and hypocrisy. He is proud of being a Hindu. But at the end, to his great shock, he finds that he is a foundling and his mother is an Irish woman. The secret is maintained till the end of the novel. Sucharita is the woman whom Gora loves. Tagore depicts her character with wonderful dexterity. Normally, two types of women found in such stories are—one motherly and another a loving mistress. The mother looks after the children, gives them milk and love too. She illumines the house as Goddess Lakshmi. The mistress arouses desire in man's heart and challenges his manly power. She makes him feel proud and confident. The mother gives him energy, and the mistress inspiration. A man needs both of these. Sucharita in *Gora* is a bold character who stands by her lover very firmly giving him advice, suggestions and consolation in his adversity.

Tagore's oft-discussed and most controversial novel is *The Home and World.* He wrote it at the time of the division of Bengal in 1905. The Bengalis thought that the division of Bengal was an attempt to break the national feeling filled with the fire of protest. This commotion was effectively depicted in *The Home and the World.* In the later novels of Tagore, the number of characters used to be the minimum. In *Home and the World* there are only three characters—the husband Nikhil, the wife Bimla and the friend Sandeep. Bimla has lived the sheltered life of a Hindu wife. Suddenly she hears the call of the outside world, when the hypocritical Sandeep inspires the national feeling in her. She is caught between the pull of her home and that of the world. Nikhil, who is the symbol of peace and security, gives her the freedom of choice. But Sandeep's luring words promise her a world of excitement and adventure, and she is carried away by the 'Krishna call' of Sandeep. It was a time of trial, error and failure for Bimla. But at last she works out her salvation diligently through tribulation and experimentation, suffering and disaster. She goes through fire and brimstone, and at last realizes the difference between gold and tinsel: 'She realizes that Nikhil has more strength and courage to face a crisis than the *Rajasik*

Sandeep who takes to heels the moment difficulties start' (*Rabindranath Tagore: A Critical Analysis*). The novel *Home and the World* is actually about the learning process of Bimla and therefore its title could better have been given as *The Education of Bimla.*

Among the Telugu novelists of the early period, Chalam has been said to be a champion of the total emancipation of women. The thrust of his fictional creations is chiefly towards an uninhabited articulation of the modern woman for emancipation. In all his novels Chalam seeks to expose the hypocrisy of the system of marriage, and champions the concept of unrestricted free love. *Daivamichchina Bharya* (The Wife Gifted by god), *Maidanam* (The Meadow), *Brahmanikam* (The Ways of the Brahmins) and *Hampi Kanyalu* (The Damsels of Hampi) are among his major novels.

The Marathi novel had its beginning in *Yamuna Paryatan* written by Baba Padmanji in 1857. But it rose to its height in the works of Harinarayan Apte (1884-1919). His novels present an unusually vivid and realistic picture of the life of the middle class. His social novel *Paan Lakshat Kongheto* is the first of its kind and still remains unsurpassed. It is cast in the form of an autobiography of a widow and is written in an exquisitely chaste and meandering style. But the story is not merely a study of the condition of Hindu widowhood of those times, but a universal cry of the individual soul struggling to rise above its environment.

It was with the intention of strengthening their hold on India that the colonial rulers encouraged English education here. They established a college at Aligarh, which subsequently became a Muslim university. As a result of the constant efforts of Sir Mirza Ahmed, education was extended to women too. A Muslim scholar called Mauli Nazir Ahmed advocated the freedom and development of women community and encouraged them to write novels and short stories. He realized that there were no books in Urdu suitable for women's reading. So he wrote six such novels, which the women would easily understand. He wrote *Mirat-ul-uroos* (A Gift to a Bride) with the intention of teaching them a good culture. The heroine of this novel is Akbari Begum—a kind, loving and soft-spoken woman. She illuminates the house of her in-laws. There is another villainous character in the novel called Azghari Begum. She destroys the peace of the whole house. Nazir Ahmed wanted the women to read this and learn from the example. After this, a women writers' tradition was developed in Urdu.

However, earlier to this, there was a male tradition in Urdu which negotiated in different ways with the institution of courtesan, cross race gender relations and the declining patronage of the Mughal Court. In 1893 Hassan Shah's novel called *Nashtar* was translated into Urdu by Sujjad Hussein Kasmandevi. In it, the male-female binary was paralleled with the white-black relationship within which the control and exercise of power was firmly placed. It had a triangular relationship. Khanum Jan is a dancing girl who has come out of her father's home because her mother has walked out of it. Khanum Jan values respectability more than anything. The young Mir-Saheb, Munshi to the British officer Ming, falls in love with her. Khanum has a fear that his master Ming would ask her to be his mistress. Therefore she demands that Mir-Saheb should marry her, at least secretly. Ming is a gentleman, but as he exercises his economic power over others; his power of control is supreme. Khanum cleverly manages to run away with Mir-Saheb. But Ming prevents her by detaining Mir-Saheb with him under some pretext. At last when the actual moment of relief comes, she is dead and buried. In this novel, issues like Khanum's attachment to respectability, her determination to connect sexuality with it, and to hold on to chastity as a condition of virtue has been beautifully presented by the author. Nowhere are the courtesans looked at with contempt. They have full freedom to visit the places of worship, to perform religious rites and learn about culture.

Mirza-Muhammed Hadi-Ruswa's *Umrao Jan Ada* (1899) is another important novel which came originally in Urdu itself. Ruswa finds a new technique to narrate the story here. The author begins it, and Umrao continues it. Thus the perceptions of her situation are both male and female. When Umrao hesitates, Ruswa prompts her by reminding her of what happened in the past. Umrao had been engaged to be married to her cousin. But she was abducted at the age of 9. She had to undergo a period of imprisonment and semi-starvation before she was sold. She becomes a courtesan and is deprived of a permanent relationship, motherhood and family life. However, as a courtesan, she had the freedom for education, learning, poetry, art and developing new relationships with the men of her choice. The entire novel runs through the description of different relationships she has entered into and she comments on the various emotional and physical requirements a woman needs for that. Her life is what she has made of it. Her choices at every stage make the readers see the values she upholds. She is different from the other courtesans in her spirit of independence. She sets up a house of her own and lives there alone without the help or support of a man.

In Punjabi, Bhai Vir Singh's novels *Sundari* and *Satwant Kaur* foregrounded the woman's control over her body and mind and the channelizing of her desires. One significant side effect of this approach was to impart a sense of dignity to the woman character, free her from the role of a sexual object (consequently from that of a wife or mistress) and raise her to the level of a helpmate or comrade. But even this approach is not modern because it emphasizes the woman's chastity and gives her a sense of agency, both within man-woman relationship and in the larger discourse of society and its concerns for survival.

The novel as a new genre took its birth in Malayalam through Appu Nedungadi's *Kundalata*. It had only the outer structure of the English novel, and did not have any good plot or characters. The curiosity it rouses is shallow and superficial, and the story itself has got some artificiality about it. Whatever be its drawbacks, it deserves the name of the first experiment in Malayalam novel.

The next novel which came following *Kundalata* was Chandu Menon's *Indulekha.* Chandu Menon had read almost all the social novels of English at that time. This gave him the inspiration to write a social novel in Malayalam, depicting the life around him. He saw the heartlessness of the land-owning Nairs and Namboothiris, their prejudices and their subsequent fall, and he wished to write about them in his novel. The orthodox rulers, who did not want to bring any reforms in the society, were made to bow their heads before Chandu Menon's work. What he had done was taking the people from the stagnation of conventionality to the chains of reality. His intention was to make any character enjoy his humour, inspire thoughts in them and develop a critical outlook in them. He never wastes even a single word in the description of any character or event.

As the name itself suggests Indulekha is the heroine of this novel. She has received English education, which was rare among the women of the times. She has a progressive outlook towards the customs and conventions of the society. That is why she raises her voice against the exploitation of women in the prevalent custom of *sambandham*—the kind of conjugal relationship between a man and a woman, without any legal security of a marriage. Indulekha takes her own decision in this regard and establishes her identity by choosing her own husband, not caring for the societal convention of *kettukalyanam* or *sambandham.*

Chandu Menon's next novel was *Sarada.* But he could not complete it before his death. It is the presentation of his experience as a magistrate. The family affairs, the displeasures, the adamant nature of the *Karanavars* (masters of matrilineal families) who instigated these quarrels, the managers of their properties who misled the *Karanavars* who did not have any practical knowledge of things, the greedy lawyers, the dependents who slavishly obeyed the orders of these *Karanavars*—all these issues are discussed in this novel. Chandu Menon discovers the thoughts and feelings, words and behaviour of all these characters getting down into their psychological depth. The *Karanavar* Kopunni Achchan gives away the beautiful young girl Kalyani to a rich, old man who was very ugly looking. He arranges this *sambandham* much against the wishes of Kalyani. But Kalyani runs away to Benares and marries an artist called Raman Menon. Sarada is their daughter. The events that take place after their return home like how they suffer, what problems they face and so on are described in the novel. Both these novels of Chandu Menon received a special recognition because at that time none of the writers dared to expose the problems of women in the society.

The realistic novels entered Tamil literature through Rajam Iyer (1872-1894). His first novel *Kamalambal Charitham* (1896) gives a realistic picture of the contrast between love of the youths and that of the elderly people. The second novel was Madhavai's *Padmavathiyin Charitham.* The reformist tendency is evidently present in it. Various episodes are intertwined and they keep developing one after another. Padmavathi's suspicion of her husband develops into a long story. Madhavai's second novel *Muthu Meenakshi*

(1903) tells the story of a young widow, narrated by herself, using the technique of an autobiography.

The first realistic novel which appeared in Kannada was Gulvadi Venkatarao's *Indirabai* or *Saddharma Vijaya* (The Victory of Righteousness). The novel attempts to bring reformation in the life of the society which has forgotten all the values. It does not develop any romantic attitude towards life, but looks at it from the practical point of view.

In the beginning, the author says that the novel deals with life history of Indirabai. But the first quarter of the novel does not say anything about her. It is filled with the cruelty and hypocrisy of her parents and their people. Her parents murder a man called Sundar Raya. Indira Bai appears in the second part of the novel. She is given in marriage to a man called Vittalraya who leads a life of promiscuity and becomes a victim to venereal diseases. He dies early and goes to live in Amritraya's house. There she meets Sundarraya's son Bhaskarraya who has returned from England after his higher studies. Bhaskarraya, with his progressive views, marries the widow Indirabai. However, the author here gives importance to chastity by saying that Indirabai has remained a virgin after her first marriage. Indirabai's character is adorned with the ideal qualities of a Victorian modern lady with English education and acquirement of softer skills.

The concept of New Woman in the early Indian fiction is region and culture specific. Each generation has produced its own version of New Woman and it gained acceptability only when it fitted into the patriarchal ideology. The regional manifestations of the versions of New Woman gave opportunity for reading different versions of modernity.

Works Cited

Aquil, Balaram and Partha Chatterjee, ed. *History in the Vernacular*. Ranikhet: Permanent Black, 2008.

Balaram, N.E. *Bharateeya Samskritika Paramparyam*. Thiruvananthapuram: Chintha Publishers, 1995.

Du Be, Leela. *Woman and Kinship: Comparative Perspectives on Gender in South and South East Asia*. Tokyo: United Nations U. P., 1997.

Jain, Jasbir. *Feminising Political Discourse: Women and the Novel in India 1857-1905*. Jaipur: Rawat, 1997.

Krishnamurthy, J., ed. *Women in Colonial India: Essays on Survival, Work and the State*. New Delhi: OUP, 1989.

Srinivas, N.N. *Social Change in Modern India*. Bombay: Allied, 1966.

Sangari, Kumkum. *Politics of the Possibli: Essays on Gender, History, Narratives and Colonial English.* New Delhi: Tulika, 1999.

Sukumar, Lakshmi. "Literary Narrative as History; The Making of the New Woman in *Indulekha* and *Parangodi Parinayam*." Kerala University: Ph.D. Thesis, 2009.

Dalit Literature in Kannada

Though the Dalit Movement in Karnataka does not have a history of more than three decades now, the concern for the Dalits and emphasis on the concept of equality are not new to Kannada literature. If we go back to the ancient poet Pampa's *Mahabharata* (10th century) we may observe the poet's genuine concern for Karna, ill-treated for being the son of a fisherman. Pampa is always remembered for his proclamation *Manushya Jaati Thanonde Valam* (*all human beings are one*). The best example for a revolt against the social discrimination based on caste system was the *Sharana* Movement which took place in the 12th century, the sole aim of which was to disintegrate the caste system and bring about equality in the society. It was during the same time that *Vachana* (aphoristic) poetry was pooled into Kannada literature by Basavanna and others, including a large number of women poets. Basavanna was an exponent of a social revolution and he worked for a society free from all sorts of discriminations. He said that the human beings should be valued for their deeds, and not for their castes.

> One who kills is a *Madiga*
> One who eats filth is a *Holeya.*
> (Madigas and Holeyas are Dalits)

T*he Vachana* poets upheld physical labour as the highest value and, argued that since the Dalits were labourers they should be uplifted and brought to the mainstream. Among the *Vachana* poets, there were Dalit women poets too, who, being illiterates, built up an oral tradition.

Sixteenth century saw the Bhakti Movement in Kannada poetry. A number of poets composed and sang poems about the importance of spirituality, as well as the values that human beings have to inculcate in their lives. These poets were called *Dasas* or, those who dedicated themselves to the service of God. All the *Dasa* poets were from the upper castes, but Kanakadasa was a Dalit poet. He was very cruelly treated by the Brahmins at Udupi Krishna Mutt. In his poetry, Kanakadasa criticizes the caste system which looks down upon the Dalits. He asks:

> Why do you fight among yourselves
> In the name of caste?
> Do you know where your caste has
> Originated from?
> What is the caste of your body?
> What is the caste of your soul?

In his *Ramadhanya Charite* also he debunks the caste system beautifully through the metaphor of Rice (The food of the rich) and Raagi (the food of the poor), establishing at the end the superiority of the latter.

The absurdity of caste system, the cruelty of the caste people, the exploitation of the lower caste people, the concept of pollution, desecration, untouchability etc. have become the themes of great Kannada writers in the subsequent periods. Shivarama Karanth's *Chomana Dudi* (Choma's Drum) is a landmark in the history of Kannada literature on Dalits. It is the heart-rending story of Choma, a Dalit, whose only desire was to own a piece of land. But, as the convention has strictly denied that right to a Dalit, his dream never gets fulfilled, and eventually he is frustrated and heart-broken. In S.L. Bhyrappa's novel *Daatu* the story tries to break the social convention by making a Brahmin woman marry a Dalit boy. Kuvempu's play *Shudratapaswi* brings out Rama's cruelty on Shambooka, who is a Shudra. U.R. Ananthamurthy's novel *Bharatipura* also discusses the protagonist's attempts to procure rights of Dalits to enter temples.

However, these writings by the educated people of the upper class, though appeared to be concerned about the Dalits, have been criticized for their utter ignorance of the actual sufferings of the Dalits. Then, in the Fifties, came the progressive writers, influenced by leftist ideology. The prominent progressive writers in Kannada were Basavaraja Kattimani, Aa. Na. Kri., Niranjana and Ta. Ra. Su. Niranjana's novel *Chirasmarane* marked the resistance against the exploitation of the downtrodden farm labourers. Kattimani's *Harijanayana* discussed the post-Independence situation of the poor. Both these works are about the denial of land to the untouchables. But they also did not touch the basic issues like untouchability, manhandling, murder, humiliation, harassment, despoliation etc. which really made the Dalits miserable. Besides, none of the above novels contains any trace of Ambedkar's principles. Instead, they exhibit their faith in Karl Marx, Gandhi or Lohia.

The *Navya* (modern) writers who came next, turned to be individualistic, and they did not bother to think of such social problems at all. It was at this time that some of the writers and thinkers with revolutionary bent of mind started the *Bandaaya* (Revolt) Movement. The aim of the *Bandaaya* Movement was to transfer the individual centred notions of the Navya writers into community-oriented thinking. Its proclamation was that all sorts of inequality in the society should be erased and progressive thinking should be made dynamic. It emphasized the social and political consciousness of a writer. This kind of a cultural organization, based on the leftist and democratic values was the first of its kind in the whole nation. Though the Progressive Movement had already spread nationwide, it had been stigmatized as a part of leftist thinking. Gandhi, Ambedkar and Lohia were not important for them. But in Bandaaya Movement all leftists, Progressive thinkers, and all those who believed in the principles of Gandhi, Ambedkar and Lohia joined together for an unequivocal fight against social inequality.

In Karnataka, Dalit and *Bandaaya* Movements went side by side. 'The Bandaaya literary organization was the house built by Dalits themselves' (Maalagatthi xi). The non-Dalit progressive writers entered into this house, assuring that they would stand as backbone to the Dalits. Gradually when the women writers, Muslim writers and others joined it, the non-Dalit progressive leaders began to argue that *Bandaaya* was a bigger circle and Dalit was a smaller one. So, it should be kept in mind that, since *Bandaaya* was a house built by Dalits themselves, at first the Dalit poetry was called *Bandaaya* poetry.

Dalit literature, with its distinctive meaning, started in the Seventies, being influenced by Marathi literature. Just as in the case of all other Indian literatures, the expression 'Dalit literature' had controversies in Maharashtra also. The old writers, who came before Ambedkar, who had shown their concern for the Dalits, never called themselves Dalit writers. However, Ambedkar's human concern, along with modern education and the influence of African Black literature brought a lot of changes in the Maharashtrian literature. This change helped the Dalits gain their self-esteem. It filled in them the spirit of fighting for justice. Consequently the Dalit Literary Association came into existence in 1948 and there was a *Dalit Writers' Conference* in 1958 in Mumbai. A memorandum was passed in it that only the literature written by the Dalit writers should be considered as *Dalit Literature*. This led to an elaborate discussion on the word 'Dalit.'

In Karnataka, the word 'Dalit*'* first came from Dharwad. In 1973, Dr. Buddhanna Hingamire, along with several others started a periodical called *Dalita* and brought out its first issue in January 1974. This was by the formation of an organization called *Dalit Pantha* (Dalit Pantheon). In the beginning of 1975, another organization called *Dalita Sangharsh Samiti* was established in Bhadravati under the leadership of B. Krishnappa. It was at the same time that 'Karnataka Barahagarara Okkoota'

(The Union of the Writers and Artists) came into existence. Both the *Dalit Sangharsh Samiti* and The Union of Writers and Artists of Karnataka collaborated to conduct a very big conference in Bhadravati on a grand scale.

In 1974, the 'Boosa Episode' of B. Basavalingappa triggered the activities of the Dalit writers. The Dalit writer Basavalingappa was giving a talk in Mysore on the new wave in Kannada literature. Referring to the traditional social system, he said that it was framed by a handful of people of the upper class and the poor had to meekly accept whatever they said. 'We have been simply caught up in it. However, the new wave tells us the way to come out of that frame. Therefore our literature has to enrich itself with such innovative findings. But what the students read in the texts today is nothing but the same dreary, worn out arguments. Our students have to read the literature of other countries, filled with revolutionary ideas and bring that wealth into Kannada. A literature without this is *Boosa* literature.' (Imraapura 434)

At first, poems and articles on Dalit life were published here and there in newspapers, magazines and periodicals. But the foundation to Dalit Literature was laid in 1975 through the publication of Siddhalingayya's *Holemaadigara Haadu* (The Song of the Holemaadigas). In fact, a book of a similar title had already been published in Telugu. At that time, Telugu literature had influenced Kannada literature so much that in 1972 an anthology of poems translated from Telugu with the title *Digambara Kavigalu* (*Naked Poets*) had been published. Besides, in 1971, the postgraduate students of Karnataka University, Dharwad, brought out an anthology of poems called *Digambara* (The Naked). In 1972, a collection of poems titled *Shudra* had been published by H. M. Patel. All these poems were pro-Dalit. The blowing of this new breeze created a congenial atmosphere for the *Holemaadigara Haadu* to make its entry. But it is to be noted here that the word 'Dalit' was not prominently seen in these poems; may be because of the influence of Karl Marx and Lohia. The one who has written his impressions about *Holemaadigara Haadu* in the anthology refers to Karl Marx, but does not mention Ambedkar in it. This hints at the poet being influenced by Karl Marx.

A large number of Dalit writers have emerged during the last 35 years. Just as in any other social movement, the path the Dalit writers have trodden so far is not a smooth one. Dalit literature, which was like the explosion of a bomb in the beginning, and made a lot of sound and fury, eventually gained ripeness and maturity, and blossomed as an art with beauty and creativity. We may list about 70 poets and more than 60 anthologies of Dalit poetry starting from Siddhalingayya. More or less 50 writers are said to have come from Dalit origin. From the writers of the first generation like Devanuru Mahadeva to the youngest writer like Hanur Chennappa, it has spread its vast canopy quite extensively. Nevertheless, it cannot claim with confidence that it has been able to depict the entire Dalit world in it. About this, what Devanuru Mahadeva himself has told in one of his interviews is noteworthy:

> I have come from a dark domain. My entry into the art medium is but an accident. What I have written so far is only some five or six fingers of man of our kingdom. At the most it may be a full hand. Still, it has been able to shake the pace of Kannada literature more than its quantity. If a few fingers can do this much, the changes that might occur when the full man of the dark domain speaks is unimaginable. (Jayaprakash 246)

The important personalities whose influence led to the prolific creation of Dalit literature in Kannada are Ambedkar, who roused the feelings of self-esteem and self-confidence among the untouchables, Rama Manohar Lohia, who awoke the Shudra consciousness, making them develop a displeasure towards the Brahmin clergy, and Gandhiji, who turned the attention of the people towards villages, Mao, who came as an inspiration to the

Naxalite activities preparing people for an armed fight, Karl Marx, who awoke class consciousness, Jyotiba Phule who nurtured the skeptical notions of people, Periyar, who made them feel disgusted towards scriptures and Vedic myths, Narayanaguru and Kudmul Rangarao who drew their attention to the untouchables.

The organizations and major events which boosted the Dalit writings were the Union of writers and Artists of Karnataka, the activities of the Karnataka *Dalit Sangharsh Samiti*, the rotten condition of Kannada Sahitya Parishad, the spate of activities of the Naxalites, the increase in the number of Non-Brahmin Associations, the activities of the Communist party, the benefits that the Dalits got from reservations, the changes in land distributions due to Land Reform Act, the Emergency creating awareness among the people, the fear in the Hindus about conversion, the increased study of folk literature, the narrow effects of the Bourgeois Liberalism of Congress, the *Boosa Episode* of Basavalingappa, the availability of Black Literature, the influence of Jayaprakash Narayan, and the growth of racism and regionalism. These influenced the people in three different ways.

At first the non-Brahmins blasted out their discontent about the Brahmins. The publicity media boosted it. A number of people started to run newspapers. Those who stood against the Brahmins managed to get entry into education and employment. The Shudras rejected the Brahmin clergy and grew strong, in the social and political fields. The *Vokkaligas and Lingayats* of Karnataka gained more importance. Among these, many of them received inspiration from Lohia. However, these intellectuals were not revolutionaries. They were just reformists and they earned the favour of the rich through their strong communist outlook. These were the limitations found in the writers who came from this class.

Secondly, a number of poor non-Brahmins got into clash with the rich Shudras. They were inspired by Marxian thinking.

However, when these poor Shudras received land when the Land Reform Act was passed, there was a sudden change in their attitude. Many of them gave up their revolutionary ideas and joined the Congress Party (e.g. a great writer like Srikrishna Alanahalli). From these thinkers, who withdrew temporarily, at least some writers were inspired. Thus the protest shown by these writers was based on economic condition, and not caste discrimination. Writers like Vishnunayaka, R.V. Bhandary, Kum. Veerabhadrappa and Baraguru Ramachandrappa fall under this category.

The third influence was related to the clash between the untouchables and the caste people. Here the untouchables had to face both the rich and the poor of the upper castes. They had been considered as completely *polluted.* The caste people wanted to sustain their policy of *pollution* even forcing the untouchables to eat faeces and establish their superiority. However, more than the crooked Brahmins, the dull-witted Shudras, who were more aggressive, could possibly cause damage to the Dalits. This made the Dalit writer, come up with his Protest *Literature.*

In the Seventies, a very large group of indignant people raised a hue and cry about the existing system and demanded a complete revolution. They wanted to break themselves away from the traditional way of life. This new class was seen all over Karnataka and they wanted to build an organization for themselves. As the traditional society did not take them into its fold, they had to separate themselves from the system which was devoid of protest. On the other hand, as they were against the ruling system too, they remained outsiders there also. The result was the formation of several progressive groups in the Seventies. The Dalits, who were with the *Bandaaya* writers in the beginning, eventually broke away from them. The protest shown by them stands on two grounds:

1. Revealing to others the details of exploitation which a Dalit has experienced in his private life in the society where he

had been born and brought up. Here the writer stands in between the exploiter and the exploited. As his protest is against the exploiter, naturally his anger is mixed with indignation. That is why it causes the displeasure and disapproval of that class. On the other hand, since he writes in favour of the exploited, it creates a feeling of self-esteem in his people. That means the source of writing of the *Dalit-Bandaaya* writers, and the direction in which it flows, stand face to face. Here the writers work as the medium of protest. Perhaps, this has restricted the creative possibility of the *Dalit-Bandaaya* writers.

2. The second type of protest is more mellowed and artistic than the first type. Here the writer is not anxious to talk about himself. Instead, he separates himself from his own class, and, turning to them once again, he tells them about themselves. Here, there is no screaming and shouting, no hue and cry, no haste, but a whisper. We have to listen to it standing at his back. We are told about the values rejected by the master-culture from a person who has come from the same culture. The same *pollution*, which has been devalued as *pollution* by the Indian traditional society, would be recorded here for the first time in letters. This recording itself is a protest. Devanuru Mahadeva is the supreme writer falling under this category.

Siddalingayya, Govindayya, Indudhara Honnapura, Munivenkatappa, Channanna Valeekara and Aravinda Malagatti are the major writers among those who articulated their feelings of protest of the former type. All of them have raised a loud cry against inequality; against the colour-caste-gender discrimination. Wrath is the essential element in them. All of them sound one and the same in the level of anger expressed in their poems. When we read all their poems, they give us the same experience. Their creativity is limited to defying the people who exploited them. Politicians and the clergy are their bitter enemies. Thus the source of their creativity is the people whom they defy; only to react to the people who stand against the poor and the Dalits. Since the very existence of these writers is due to the existence of their exploiters, they cannot grow beyond their first anthology of poems of stories. Had they moved forward keeping their own life as their ground, their protest would have acquired different dimensions. A writer, who lacks the actual experience of life, however firm ideologically, is not able to show the signs of growth.

Siddhalingayya's anthology of poems called *Holemaadigara Haadu* (1975) is the first of its kind in *Dalit-Bandaaya* protest literature. A mixed feeling of indignation and regret could be seen in the poems 'Nanna Janagalu' (My People), 'Ondu Mooleya Hadu' (The Song of a Bone), 'Ondu Padya Kranthi Pada' (The Song of a Poetic Revolution), 'Habba' (Festival), 'Masanada Cheluve' (The Pretty Woman of the Graveyard). Some samples of his lines:

> Those who paid interest, those who burnt to ashes,
> On the fire of speeches—are my people
> Those who ate *paramannam* in the name of God
> Those who stitched boots and slippers
> —are my people. ('Nanna Janagalu')

> They allow the dog which eats our faeces inside
> They eat what we grow and take what we labour
> But us they do not want
> Instead of calling us *Holeyas* and *Madigas*
> Ah! they call us *Harijans*, and laugh at us.
> ('Ondu Padyada Kranthi)

Siddhalingayya has shown his protest in umpteen such lines, expressing his genuine feelings. Outrightly rejecting the individual-centred perspective of *Navya* literature, he began to write from the perspective of the community. And the language that he used for it was the Bandaaya language. His second anthology was *Saviraaru Nadigalu* (Thousands of Rivers). Since the protest shown here carries the dream of a revolution, it is more matured than the first one. The lines that beat the inertia, dullness and weariness of the world, exhibit the sense of responsibility to protect the health of the world. It is not a mere record of the injustice done to them in the contemporary society, it suggests some alternative too. The undaunted courage, confidence and radiance in them lend an artistic beauty to the protest.

> Dark face, silver beard and burning eyes
> They kicked off their sleep slitting the days and nights
> Their blankets felt sorry, with those who got up.
> When they danced, there was an earthquake.
> The roaring tigers and lions crept in a row like ants.
> Down, down inequality! ('Saviraaru Nadigalu')

This poem reveals the unlimited energy that may be there within the exploited, and it rejects the present altogether. This petulance itself is a protest here. The other poems in this anthology also show the agility and life hidden in the exploited. The poet is indignant towards the system which has suppressed it. He says:

> With crores and crores of dreams
> With burning and flaming minds
> In the proclamation of thunder and lightening
> In the language of earthquakes
> Ho! there came the procession of the Dalits
> Writing on the ground with their feet. ('Saviraaru Nadigalu')

Siddalingayya, who has stuck the design of revolution to the expression of protest, is a person who has cherished the dreams of an alternative culture. It was possible for Kannada Poetry to envisage the maximum protest through the balance which he achieved between the intellectual framework and artistic expression.

The poets who came after Siddhalingayya, since they involved themselves in reacting against the upper caste or upper class people, some kind of monotony was seen in their protest.

Many of them failed to bring revolutionary changes in language and imagery. Some writers, who could plunder from experience, have been able to show protest effectively in their first anthologies. Some of them are:

Coming they are coming
The shoes that we stitched
Coming to our colony
Vanish unseen with the silver stars.
(Aravinda Maalagatthi, 'Jogathi Kallu' [The Stone of Jogathi])

Throughout his anthology *Mookanige Bai Bandaaga* (When the Dumb Could Speak), Araavinda Malagathi has written significant poems like this. He has expressed his protest, revealing things from within Dalit world. But later, this same protest, separated from the Dalit world, restricted itself to mere curses and abuses. Therefore, his other anthology *Kappu Kaavya* (Black Poetry) does not give the intensity of experience given by the first one. In it, only his reaction to the upper caste and upper class is recorded. Only in a poem like 'Meravanige Haadu' (The Song of Procession) he has created a new metaphorical language to express his displeasure:

Procession of silence for this
Step of our revolution
Procession of torches made of bones and skins
To the burning earth
To our song without words
Voice is the air that we breathe
No music of the rhythm of drums
The eyelids themselves are rhythms. ('Meravanige Haadu')

Here the poet has expressed his protest by relying on silence, embracing breath and giving up words, taking the rhythms of eyelids instead of the rhythm of drums:

The sample lines of protest in other poets are:
If you shake your legs off a little bit

The chains won't break, but
The Milky Way will appear in the sky
If you struggle a little bit to break your silence
Words won't come out, but
The ground itself will sing breaking its heart. (Chandrashekhara Patil, 'Ondaanondu Kalakke' [For Once upon a Time])

O Death!
Whenever I think of you
I feel like catching hold of
The poisonous minded who kill
Supporting inequality and,
Give them to you. (Ramjan Darga, 'Saave!' [O Death!])

In these huts now
Burning hot
The fire balls are
Getting ready
Will explode, finding time.
(Basavaraja Sabarada, 'Astitva' [Existence])

Do not kill us with silence
We do not want pity.
We do not want maths book.
Silver cuffs, arithmetic
Stand up shaking spider legs
Plan to say few words.
Be friends with life-giving blend head and heart.
(Baragur Ramachandrappa, 'Ontidani' [Lone Voice])

Still when our ever obedient poor donkey
Bursts with indignation seldom at least
Gets suffocated and kicks off
Joining its strong legs together.
(Kalegowda Nagaavara, 'Katte Basava' [Donkey Bull])

Throw away the scriptures into hell
That do not teach human religion
The live-scripture is enough that brings
The awareness that

> That all human beings are same. (Chennanna Valeekara, 'Yuvajanangada Hadu' [The Song of the Youth])
>
> The breathless people sang the song when
> The stars were dead and the moon was dim
> The moonlight reeked of rotten corpse
> The cuckoos fell dead flapping their wings
> Drinking poison. (Purushothama Bilimale, 'Usirilladavaru Pada Haadidaru' [The Breathless Sang the Song])

The above lines exhibit the varieties as well as limitations of protest. In the poems of women poets like S. Usha, Vijaya Dabbe, Madhavi Bhandari, Gudibande Poornima, Kamala Hemmige, Mukthayakka, B.T. Lalitha Nayak, Vijayashree Sabarada and Shashikala Vastrada also protest of the same vein could be seen. As their protests seem to be a reaction against the upper caste and upper class, they lack the immensity of the grassroots.

The protest seen in *Dalit-Bandaaya* poetry was seen in other genres also. In the short stories and novels of Baraguru Ramachandrappa, Ka. Ta. Chikkanna, Besagarahalli Ramanna, R.V. Bhandary, Rajashekhara Neeramanvi, Indudhara Hoppapura, Sathisha Kulakarni, S. Divakar, Janagere Venkataramayya, Kalegowda Naagavaara, C.V. Pateel, Channanna Valeekara, S.S. Hiremath etc. the dignity and honour of a human being, the ideal of individual freedom and the spirit of self-esteem are held high.

The novels of Baragur describe the feudal system alive even now in the post-Independence Indian villages. Baragur depicts the protest coming from within that system in a romantic manner. In such cases, it sounds as though the writer's Marxist views are being imposed on the structural assumption of villages. The Gowda in the novel *Soothra* (Trick), landlord Kelageppa in *Huttha* (The Anthill), Basayya of *Ondu Oorina Kathe* (The Story of a Village)—all symbolize the tyranny of feudalism. Parvati and Rajanna Master, Sanjeeva and, Maara—symbolize protest. In *Ondu Oorina Kathe* the entire system collapses because of the internal weakness in the system itself. In the midst of all these, sexuality and political powers become the source of torture and violence. As the famous critic D.R. Nagaraj rightly says: 'Baragur's works have more or less cardboard characters.' (Nagaraj 10) Though his views are progressive, as they are monotonous in their themes, they lose their lustre.

The protest in Mulluru Nagaraj's novel *Marana Mandala Madhyadolage* (In the Middle of the Circle of Death) also looks simple. Only Kalegowda Naagavaara is a little different. His perseverance is searching for the meaningful and lasting values of unstained love which crosses the barriers of caste and class is an immense protest against the trivialities of the times.

Thus the protest shown by all of them are of the same nature. In short, it was a collective effort. Its effect was such that, unlike in the *Navya* Movement, a single poet could not be called the representative poet. This is a rare achievement made by the *Dalit-Bandaaya* literature. It did not give rise to any 'feudal lord' in Dalit poetry.

The writers who showed their protest of the second type, like Devanuru Mahadeva, were free from the flaws seen in those of the first type. Hence, justice is done and balance is maintained in the protest here. Besagarahalli Ramanna, Chaduranga, Poornachandra Thejaswi and Kum. Veerabhadrappa are closer to this category. They record the condition of the lower castes and classes in an indiscriminate way and bring out the unfathomable spirit hidden within them as well as their dreams.

Kum. Vee. (Kum. Veerabhadrappa) has done it very efficiently. He is more concerned about registering the culture rejected by the present society and the revolt rising from the same point. He collects the particulars of the lower class life, which are unknown to the middle class readers, in his stories like *Kappu* (Black), *Beli Mattu Hola* (Fence and Field), *Kattalanu Thrishula Hidida Kathe* (*The Story of Thrishula Catching Darkness*), *Kivuda Naayiyada Prasanga* (The Episode of the Deaf

Becoming a Dog), *Doma Eluganemba Koraganu Chavudanemba Handiyu* (A Koraga called Eluga, and a Pig named Chavuda) using a folk dialect of the Kottur region in Bellary District. The characters who appear in his stories are not the ones who come only to fight. Instead they symbolize a race. The creativity and love of life that these people exhibit flash like lightening, despite their poverty, unemployment and exploitation. Kum Vee. becomes closer to Devanuru here itself. His recording of culture which is being suppressed and marginalized by the ruling class becomes a powerful protest here.

The difference between Kum. Vee. and Devanur is seen in their way of ending their stories. Kum Vee's stories end in a romantic way. But Devanur's is a calm and composed way, as though he is administering consolation to his own people. Most of the Dalit writers react to the upper class; but Devanuru deals with the Dalit world itself, using a language which is closer to his own experience. On the whole, Devanur's writings are the best models of protest literature. In all his stories and novels, we can find the twin extremes of birth-death, love-lust, quarrel-fighting, festival, drinking and merry making. These are not restricted to the cry that all of them have been exploited. Instead, they draw our attention to the different faces of life. About his most acclaimed novella *Odalaala* (The Depth of One's Hunger), U.R. Ananthamurthy says:

> After inevitably moving away from his native place when he writes this narrative, this action of writing itself is an action of regaining what he has lost, and regaining his own people's love and affection. When the Harijan family eats groundnuts sitting round the fire, shining in the brilliance of the fire, and when the peacock dances after drawing Gowri, when Sakavva tells stories to Shivu, and when the Harijan women laugh on seeing P.C. Revanna pissing—the love that the author feels for these characters becomes ours too. They and we become one. Not in pity, but in involvement. They become examples for man's irrepressible spirit. As we

> begin to think how much full-of-life are these Harijans, the narrative inspires us to think how unlimited would have been the possibility of their energy, had they overcome their poverty. That is why the protest here does not become trivial. Instead, it becomes the power to win over the conflicts of terrible reality. (108-11)

Dyavanuru is the anthology of seven short stories by Devanuru Mahadeva. He has called them episodes. Though without any symbols and images, they are not easily understandable stories. Beera of the story 'Maarikodavaru' (Those who Sold Themselves Out), when he comes to learn that his pretty wife Lachumi has illicit relationship with his master's son Kittappa, having no other alternative, adjusts himself to the situation because his feeling of gratitude to his master, who has given him food and shelter, stands as an obstacle. The Gowda of the story *Grastharu* (The Affected) thinks that the one who has taken his help should remain ever grateful to him, but the helped person defies him. Beera of *Maarikondavaru* is from within the Dalit community, whereas the person in *Grastharu* is from the upper class. In the story 'Ondu Dahanada Kathe' (The Story of a Cremation) there is the depiction of the octopus grips of social conventions. When Chikkanna marries a woman from another caste, against the wishes of his parents and the caste people of the village, they object to his participation in the cremation of his grandmother. The last story in this anthology is *Amasa*. It depicts the process of growth of an orphan called Amasa. There is the picturesque description of *Maari* festival celebrated by the Dalits. None of these stories has got *Dyavanuru* as its title. The title may be because the stories are woven around the life at the village of Dyavanuru. This anthology draws our attention particularly because of its use of colloquial language without changing even a little bit of its freshness and originality.

'Odalaala' (The Depth of Hunger) is not only the best narrative by Devanuru, but the best one in the whole of Kannada literature itself. It reminds us of the writings of Chinua Achebe. The life of miseries of a Dalit family is the central theme of the novel. Its poverty, hunger, desires and ambitions, human relationships, family feuds—the author puts before us a small world of Dalits describing how they are being hurt, insulted and exploited by the upper class. Though there is a touch of humour in the narrative, the feeling of regret behind it does not go unnoticed. It gives a different dimension to the story. The entire story runs round the single incident of the Dalit woman Saakavva's fowl being lost and her unending search for it. Though she gives a complaint to the police about it, they do not do anything for her. All the eight members of Saakavva's house have not eaten anything for four-five days, so one of her sons steals a small bag of groundnuts from the landlord's house. When the angry landlord tells the police about it, they come to Saakavva's house to catch her son red-handed. But by the time the police enter their hut, they had finished eating it. Though this can be called the skeleton of the story, the intermittent pictures add a lot to the total effect.

Kusumabaale is Devanur's full-fledged novel. In its theme, language and presentation it has erased the line of separation between the oral and written tradition. At the same time it has caught the special qualities of folk and classical art. Love and sexual relationships between several pairs of men and women—Dalits and upper castes—is seen throughout the novel trying to establish the view that all the caste barriers should be obliterated. G.S. Amur rightly says: This novel has got the fourth dimension suggested by Wole Soyinka, i.e. relieving the Dalits from exploitation and calling it a complete life.' Viewed from this perspective, we feel that *Kusumabaale* neatly depicts one single context in the life of the Dalits in its relation with all others.

Aravinda Malagatthi's novel *Kaarya* (Funeral Rites) has come out of the observation of Dalit culture. The novel moves around the funeral rites of a Dalit woman called Bangaravva. Through the different incidents and situations, the author has attempted throughout to show how tradition could be cruel and heartless for the Dalits. There is no direct protest here. The form of this novel resembles poetry. The narrative tells about the contrast between what one wishes and what really happens. The funeral rites which actually have to take place on the third day get postponed to fifth day. The flock of crows which should have come together for the offering of the *Pinda* (the ball of rice) flock round Bangarvva's dead body which drops out of the tomb. Thus time and situation go beyond 'tradition' and the novel points at the inevitability of the people in this environment trespassing the tradition.

Another novel which draws our attention is *Maagi* by Ma. Na. Javarayya. It gives the vast details of Dalit culture. The protagonist of this novel is Maagi or Maagavva, a buoyant woman with bubbling enthusiasm for life. She has the capacity to grow, tolerating all pains. She has been depicted as the fountain of Dalit energy. The novel gives deep insights into Dalit life. There is no protest here, but only a strong fight for life. The character of Maagi, who puts up with all the tortures given to her by all at home, even by her own children, fighting against all adverse circumstances with stunning equanimity, has been sketched by the author with great care.

Belya, *Huligemma*, *Kote Bagilu* (Entrance to the Fort), *Ondu Hennina Olajagattu* (A Woman's Inner World) are the novels of Channanna Valeekara, a noteworthy Dalit writer of Hyderabad. He has used the dialect of the Dalits of Raichur District for his first novel *Belya.* However, the difficulty of communication kept it away from the readers. His second novel *Huligemma* is the story of a beautiful Dalit woman who falls a victim to the lust of the upper class people. In his next novel *Ondu Hennina Olajagattu*, he has tried to unravel the psyche of an upper caste woman who falls in love with a Dalit.

Mogalli Ganesh, Amaresh Nugadoni and Prahlad Agasanakatte are the three major Dalit writers who came to limelight in the nineties. Mogalli Ganesh made his entry into the Kannada literary world through his anthology of short stories *Buguri* (Top). In his first anthology itself he has drawn the attention of the readers through his sensitive description of the details of Dalit life, the originality of the dialect spoken by them, their wretched condition, and the atrocities done on them by the so-called upper class. His later anthologies are *Mannu* (The Soil) and *Kannemale* (The Virgin Forest)

The number of plays written by Dalit writers in Kannada is very small. It is because, at the time when the Dalit writers came up with their protest literature, the Kannada theatre was busy producing the plays of New Wave. Consequently, the Dalit plays were not brought to stage. They had to remain either as street plays or as closet-reading plays. Among the published plays we have *Panchama* (The Fifth One) *Nelasama* (The Demolished) and *Ekalavya* by Siddhalingayya, *Samudradolagana Uppu* (The Salt inside the Sea) by Aravinda Malagathi, *Dalitana Mataantarada Prasanga* (The Episode of the Conversion of a Dalit) by L. Hanumanthayya. *Chaja* describes the way in which the power of exploitation is born within the Dalits and it is built round the life of a woman. *Kendamandala* depicts the inner conflict of a Dalit who comes to a city and lives as a New-Brahmin. *Ekalavya*, *Panchama* and *Nelasama* tell that knowledge or education should do good to the society and should not be misused. *Ekalavya* proclaims that the knowledge of archery is meant only for the protection of the forest.

'Dalit autobiographies are monuments of humiliation and self-esteem.' (Malagatthi xvi) The Dalit autobiographies in Kannada are limited to the student days of those writers. They are written in their declining age. The main aim of these autobiographies is not just recording, but a social revolution. So, the things which are complementary to it only have become their themes. None of them is in the form of a diary, or a record of memories. They have come up making it a rule that the articulation of matured thinking is prohibited to autobiographies. The renowned Kannada critic D. R. Nagaraj had already stipulated that in Kannada, there is a cultural resistance to an honestly written autobiography, written at an adult age. But the Dalit autobiographies break this rule.

Four Dalit autobiographies have been published in Kannada so far. *Manegaara* (Revenue Inspector) and *Oorukeri* (Village-Colony) find their place in the vision of a life of struggle. In *Manavilladavana Madhye* (Amidst the Mindless) very personal experiences take prominence. But it draws our attention by its bulk. In *Government Brahmana* the investigatory mind of the Dalit is seen.

Thumbadi Ramayya's *Manegaara* stands different among the Dalit autobiographies because of its picturesque description and its style of presentation in a pleasant tone. He never raises his voice; never goes to glorify any episode. The sincerity is kept through the work.

Oorukeri is the much acclaimed autobiography of Siddhalingayya. It has two parts. According to the list of contents *Oorukeri* is the first part. The second part is D.R. Nagaraj's backword titled *The Power of Laughter of the Poor*. There are 5 chapters in the autobiography: 1) First days of joining School, 2) School Days, 3) Hostel Life, 4) College Life and 5) Various progressive Forums.

There is a question why the Dalit writers in Kannada articulated their feelings and experiences only through poetry, short stories and novels. Aravinda Malagatti's autobiography *Government Brahm*ana came as an answer to this. Malagatti has unravelled the expanse of his experience in a very natural style here. This work has created a stir in the entire cultural thinking in Kannada. However, only the experiences of the author till he reached the age of adulthood are narrated here. That too, his childhood days and days at school and college. Just like many other autobiographies, *Government Brahmana* also is not the life history of an individual. It is a comment on the conventions, beliefs and customs of a society based on caste differences, a society which is blissfully unaware of the hunger of human beings as hunger, which does not recognize their feelings as feelings and which does not accept their love as love.

In Siddhalingayya's *Oorukeri* the ironic tone that beats throughout is stunning. He says:

> My autobiography is not the story of my experience alone. This is the narrative of the experiences of the Dalit world. Thus it is a narrative which hides the dark dreams of this dumb world in thousands of minds. I am only their mouthpiece. So, it is echoing, breaking the walls of different languages of the readers' hearts. When the story of the entire dumb world, the dreams collected in literature begin to blossom, the dumb world will become one with the world of light; and then only there will be a transformation.

Feminism should be discussed from a social perspective. When the protest of the Dalits is against the inequality in the society, it may look absurd if the Dalit women stand against the inequality found within their community. But the question should not be looked from a narrow perspective that Dalit feminism is related to their internal matters. Instead of taking it as the cleaning of the interior of their homes it should be considered as the cleaning of their yards. The internal purification provides the moral courage to fight against the external problems. Therefore Dalit feminism should be considered as an instrument to filter their own society.

Is it necessary to do this classification from within? Of course, women in general are suffering from exploitation. Particularly, the upper caste women are more exploited by the beliefs and customs that have been practised down the ages. The upper caste women are denied the economic and social freedom which the Dalit women are enjoying. This has become a topic of discussion among the feminists. Since the women writers representing the Dalits, who could write authoritatively, are very few, the real problems of Dalit women have not come to light.

In a caste-based country like India, an internal classification of feminism is inevitable. Since the Dalits did not have any social freedom, when they lived a miserable life, the Dalit women getting economic and social freedom within the family was a part of her helplessness. This internal freedom of the Dalit women became convenient for the non-Dalit community to do atrocities on her. Therefore the Dalit woman was able to get more exploited by the non-Dalit men as well as women. She became a donkey, working outside as well as inside home. Besides, there were other fundamental questions like the beliefs prevalent in the Dalit community about a woman's association with Gods. It was she who was always 'possessed.' The religious beliefs and customs discriminated between a Dalit man and a woman. She was the victim to systems like *Jogavva*, *Devadasi* etc. Most of the times, it was the Dalit woman who was molested in broad daylight. These questions are to be discussed by the Dalit feminist writers.

Sukanya Maruthi, Mallika Ghanti, B.T. Lalita Nayak, Dharanidevi Malagatti are some of the Dalit women poets. Among them, B.T. Lalita Nayak is the leading name. She belongs to the backward Lambani community. She started her literary enterprise with the writing of poems. Subsequently she shifted herself to other genres like short stories and novels. As she grew up with the *Dalit-Bandaaya* resistance, one could see the revolting spirit in her works. Her first novel *Nele-Bele* (1980) discusses the constant exploitation, insult and injustice heaped upon women in the male-dominated society. However, when compared to her subsequent novel *Gathi Nele-Bele* looks rather immature in its treatment and theme. In *Gathi*, the heroine attacks patriarchy which treats woman as a second rate citizen. She is exploited by her drunkard husband and her jealous in-laws. If she remains barren she alone is blamed for it and her sufferings are two-fold. In *Gathi* Lalita Nayak has given a touching description of the blind beliefs, meaningless customs, life-killing superstitions, exploitation of the Dalit women by the Brahmin clergy in the name of God and religion, illiteracy and poverty.

Geeta Nagabhooshan is another major woman writer whose short stories and novels open a new vista of Dalit women's miseries. Her novel *Baduku* (Life), which has won her the Central Sahitya Akademi Award, is a heartrending narrative describing Dalit life. B.T. Jahnavi and Dr. Vinaya also have drawn the attention of the Kannada critics through their short stories on Dalit life.

Though Dalit literature in Kannada has come a long way, bringing up more than a hundred major and minor poets, short story writers, novelists and playwrights, a major critic has not come up so far. For criticism, since Dalit literature has depended on the non-Dalit critics so far, a separate class of Dalit critics could not develop. However, today it has realized the need for developing a line. Those who stood as an inspiration to the creation of Dalit literature in the beginning, since they joined politics, there was none to take initiative. Some of them began to think that, for evaluating Dalit literature, Dalit thinkers should come up. Eventually, Karnataka Sahitya Akademi published two books—*Dalita Kavya* and *Dalita Kathegalu*. However, these anthologies limited the concept of Dalits to scheduled castes and scheduled tribes. Had the earlier publications *Bandaaya Kaavya* and *Bandaaya Kathegalu* been named as *Dalit-Bandaaya* the question of segregation would not have been raised. But that was due to the politics of non-*Dalit-Bandaaya* writers. This has made the Dalits now think that there is a need for moving beyond the government centered interpretation, thinking that, otherwise, the Dalit Movement will not survive for long.

Works Cited

Amur, G.S. *Devanurara Kusumabaale*. Bangalore: Prajavani, 1988.

Ananthamurthy, U.R. "Devanuru Mahadevara *Odalaala*," *Sahitya Vimarshe*, ed. T.P. Ashoka. Bangalore: Karnataka Sahitya Akademi, 1983: 108-11.

Ashoka, T.P. *Devanurara 'Odalaala.' Dalita Maarga*, ed. Aravinda Maalagatthi. Bangalore: Kannada Pustaka Praadhikara, 2002: 357-59.

Bilimale, Purushothama. *Dalita-Bandaaya Sahitya Prathibhatane; Abhivyakthi. Dalita Maarga*, ed. Aravinda Maalagatthi. Bangalore: Kannada Pustaka Praadhikara, 2002: 129-52.

Imrapura, Somashekhar. *Basavalingappa Avarondige Sandarshana. Dalita Maarga*, ed. Aravinda Maalagatthi. Bangalore: Kannada Pustaka Praadhikara, 2002: 434-36.

Jayaprakash, Banjagere. "Kathasahityadalli Dalitathe mattu Ambedkar," *Vichaara Sahitya*, ed. H.T. Pothe. Bangalore: Karnataka Sahitya Akademi, 2007: 244-51.

Maalagatthi, Aravinda. *Prasthaavane. Dalitamaarga*, ed. Aravinda Maalagatthi. Bangalore: Kannada Pustaka Praadhikara, 2002, ix-xxx

Naagaraj, D.R. *Amritha mattu Garuda*. Bangalore: Pustaka Chandana, 1983.

Rai, Vivek B.A. *Adbhutha Saankethika Kaavya*: Kaarya. Dalita maarga, ed. Aravinda Maalagatthi. Bangalore: Kannada Pusthaka Praadhikaara, 2002, 372-74.

Siddhalingayya. *Oorukeri*. Sagara: Akshara Prakaashana, 1996.

Vijayashankar, S.R. *Devanurara Kusumabaale*. Dalita Maarga, ed. Aravinda Maalagatthi. Bangalore: Kannada Pusthaka Praadhikaara, 2002; 360-63.

Dialectics of Translation as Transcreation

The advanced technology in communication has gained a lot of importance in recent years. As a result of this, the linguistic barriers among different parts of the world are shrinking to a great extent. Much attention is given by everyone, learned as well as laymen, to acquire more knowledge about the affairs of the world today. In this context, very significantly, translation has occupied an important role for a better and easier means of understanding the affairs of the world. The progress going on all around us, in the neighbouring states as well the distant countries, in various spheres, has attracted the attention of everyone, thereby necessitating translation more than ever before.

Translation has subsumed different meanings under different contexts, and therefore, the terminological definition of translation, inclusive of all those meanings is a difficult task. Rendering the literature of one language in another language is its superficial lexical interpretation. But it does not solve the epistemological problem of such literature as is available in translation.

The concept of translation is not new to the Indians, though how it has come to be practised in the present context is of western origin. In India, in very old days too, the practice of translation existed, though in a different way. That was how our great writers in regional languages, wrote their important poetical works, based on the stories available in ancient literary works in Sanskrit like the *Ramayana* and the *Mahabharata*. That could be called idea—based translation. Taking the ideas from the original works, they developed the whole story in their own style and language. When the westerners came to India and studied Sanskrit with the purpose of taking its rich, ancient literature to the west, some amount of latitude became inevitable for them because of the linguistic, stylistic and cultural variation. Daniel H.H. Ignall's translation of Vidyakara's *Subhashitha Rathna Kosha*, J. Massan and B.K. Matilal's translation of *Yogavasishtaramayana*, William Jones' *Saccontala* could be given as examples for the liberty taken by translators, which, in fact, made their works 'transcreations.'

It is with the advancement made in the field of Linguistics that translation came to be more text based, because, in the idea-based translation, there was very little scope for the infusion of cultural entities of the original work. As any language is inseparable from its culture, whenever it is translated into another language, if it is text based, there will be a better scope for an understanding between the two language groups. With this purpose in view, there has been an abundant surge of translation works among the European languages after Renaissance. Still, the experience of the translators has proved that 100% translation is impossible. Some allowance has to be made for the translators to claim some freedom which helps them strike a fine balance between free rendering and precise translation. Transcreation is possible here also.

Before going into the problems of translation, let us at the very outset confirm to ourselves, what fundamentally the purpose of translation is. No doubt it acts as a link between two worlds. If we consider a language as representing a cultural world, translation builds up a relationship between two worlds. Translation becomes necessary because of the instinctive curiosity in people to learn about others and develop a relation with them. Learning about others and understanding them may lead one day to develop a bond with them too. Thus translation becomes useful and it makes our lives fruitful. Hence, a translator's profession is a noble one. It is a humanity-friendly job.

However, to do justice to his/her job, he/she should dedicate himself/herself entirely and work very hard on it. When you look at translation through history all over the world, you may see that the translators had been placed next to the original writers. But the fact is that a translator is superior because he/she should be thorough with the full knowledge of the two cultural worlds, without being what, he/she will not be successful in his/her attempt. For achieving this, he/she should be constantly in touch with the language and culture of the two worlds he/she deals with.

However, in spite of being ever alert, the translator faces problems which are indispensable as far as the cultural issues are concerned. These problems are not limited to novels alone, but poetry, drama and several other prose writings too face the same hurdles. These problems arise not only because of cultural difference, but also linguistic expressions. I have faced these problems while translating from Malayalam to Kannada and vice versa, and more so in the case of English to Kannada and vice versa.

The major causes of translation problems in all languages are non-coincidences between the two languages, differing environments and difference in cultural contexts. These problems could be classified as external and internal. The external problems are those connected with language and culture. Language, which is the medium of communication, is an instrument which acts according to Time and Space. That means, it is faithful to Time and Space, and constantly undergoes changes. Change in form, meaning and tone may be seen in the same language from place to place and time to time. The similarities, which we see in languages which belong to different linguistic families, are only coincidental. The translator should be careful about it.

The problems related to language are subdivided as lexical and grammatical. Those related to form, meaning and tone are lexical, and those related to sentence and subject matter are grammatical. The first and foremost problem in translation is comprehension and expression. If you have an excellent hold on both the languages, the translation would achieve excellence. Otherwise, it will be crippled. If the knowledge of the source language is raw, translation will be poor. I can give you a few examples:

i) Satish, how long are you going to stay here?
ii) The programme was put off.
iii) You should think of me now and then.

An improper knowledge of the idiomatic expressions used here like *how long, put off, now and then,* will make the translator go wrong in translation. This, in fact, is the defect of the translator, and it disqualifies him/her as a translator. It is not translation problem. Problems are faced in translation, only when the translator fully understands everything in the source language, and finds it difficult to articulate the same in the target language.

To find out the meanings of words, usually we refer to dictionaries of both source and target languages. However, a translator should be careful here also. The dictionary is the list of meanings seen by its writer only during the time of its publication. Since the meanings of words keep changing from time to time, the editor of a dictionary enlists the various meanings of a word identified till then. In historical dictionaries, sometimes the years of a change in meaning also are given. In spite of this, sometimes, the changed meanings may not be recorded. An improper scrutiny on the part of the editorial board may miss the entry of new meanings. Consequently, the dictionary might give you some other meaning to you, which is wrong in your context. For example, the Oxford English dictionary gives the meaning of the word *elephantiasis* as 'the name given to various kinds of cutaneous diseases, which produce in the part, affected a resemblance to elephant's hide.' But everybody now knows that elephantiasis is not a skin disease. Thus the translator should take extra care while selecting meanings from the dictionary. Among the several meanings given in the dictionary, choosing which meaning suits your context is left to your discretion. Very often, we may not get an apt word in the dictionary. In such cases, the context itself should decide the word, and here the translator's creativity should come to his/her help. He/she has to create new words by giving a new turn to the old word.

In the case of translating from one regional language into another, a problem may arise in the usage of certain words. These words may be having the same form and pronunciation in the two languages, but their meanings and the contexts in which they are used may be entirely different. When a Malayalam novel is translated into Kannada or vice versa, a translator comes across such words. For example:

Anuvada in Kannada means 'translation,' but in Malayalam it means 'permission.' *Avasara* in Kannada means 'haste' but in Malayalam it means 'opportunity.' *Avakasha* in Kannada means 'chance' or 'space' but in Malayalam it means 'right.' Hundreds of such examples could be given for this. If a translator does not give attention to the change in these meanings, he /she will be a miserable failure, spoiling the whole effect.

Semantic equivalence should be achieved by following certain rules. Though the dictionary gives us the meanings, we should understand that no word in this world is an exact substitute for the other, because each word is coined in different contexts, and hence have different shades of meanings. This becomes a problem to us when we translate from or to the other languages. Some words we can keep as they are, if they are proper nouns. But if certain adjectives or attributes are found, like *peethambaradhari* or *gajacharmambara* we have to explain the word, referring to an already familiar word like 'one who wears yellow colour cloth' or 'one who wears the elephant skin.' This kind of translation is called 'merging.' After once giving such explanation, we may use it as it is in the source language. *Yugadi*, *Deepavali*, *Khadi* etc are some such examples.

Idiomatic expressions, phrases and proverbs are the living signs of a language. If you make use of them, properly understanding their meaning and suitability, they strengthen the effect of the language. But, if you fail to understand, you will be the butt of laughter too. For example, a phrase like 'put up.' If you literally translate it as *mukalil vekkuka* (in Malayalam) or *mele idu* (in Kannada) it will be a non-sense. In the case of translation from Hindi, mistakes might occur as follows:

If you translate *Hava se baten karna* as *kattinotu samsarikkuka* (in Malayalam) or *gaaliyondige Mathanaduvudu* (in Kannada) it is wrong. It should be *vegam oduga* (in Malayalam) or *bega odu* (in Kannada). For *bhag liya* in Hindi, if you say *pankeduththu* (in Malayalam) or bhagavahisida (in Kannada) it is wrong. It should be *olichchodi* (in Malayalam) or *odi hoda* (in Kannada). For *danton tale oongali dabayi* in Hindi if you say *pallinte mel viral vechchu* in Malayalam it is wrong. It should be *albhuthappettu* or *moogina mele beralitta* in Kannada.

However, there are certain phrases and idioms which could be translated just as they are, without losing their meanings. Like, for example, crocodile tears, lion's share, throw dust into someone's eyes, bird's eye view, move heaven and earth etc. But, if such a translation is not possible, their verbal or literal translation leads to a wrong interpretation. Therefore, at first you have to look for its meaning, and then try to find out a similar expression in the target language, because all languages have such idioms and phrases, to be used in the same contexts, only using different words. If you rightly find it out, that method is called assimilation. For example, a phrase like *Herculean task*, meaning some very difficult task, could be phrased in Kannada and Malayalam as *harasahasam.*

When you translate a proverb you should see that your words successfully bring out its meaning as well as tone. If you put *All that glitters is not gold* as *minnunnathella ponnalla* (in Malayalam) meaningwise it is not wrong. But if you say, *veluththittullathellam palalla* its tone comes out more effectively.

The central part of the translation exercise is syntax or the sentence construction. For this, you should be familiar with the method of constructing sentences both in the source and target languages. In all Indian languages, we do not see much difference in the order of subject, verb and object of a sentence. But in English it is entirely different. What comes at the beginning of an English sentence comes at the end or middle of a sentence in our regional language. If I say 'I came to Kalaty from Kundapura by train yesterday to participate in a seminar on Translation Studies,' you put it in Malayalam as *Njan Kundapurathilninnu Kalatyilekku Vivarthana pathanaththe kurichu oru seminaril panketukkan innale vandiyil eththichchernu* or in Kannada as *Naanu Kundaapuradinda Kalatige bhashanthara Adhyayanada kurithu ondu seminarinalli bhaagavahisalu railinalli ninne bande.*

The sentence structures in English are classified as exocentric and endocentric. A structure which is clear in itself, which does not need any explanation in another context is endocentric. However, some sentences, in the context of another tradition or culture, need a different explanation altogether, because they are comprehensible only in a particular context. Such structures are exocentric. In a way, proverbial usages, metaphors and certain words used in different branches of study are exocentric. For example, a word like 'latitude.' It has got different meanings in Geography, Physics and Literature. In Literature, it means 'freedom to choose the way you do something.' So, without fixing the word in the proper context, you cannot translate it.

Normally, the sentences in English are long. There will be the principal clause either preceded or succeeded by several subordinate clauses, and sometimes by parenthetical clauses. But when we translate the sentence into our regional language, if we do not make proper changes in the sentence structure, it may look very odd. After reading the full sentence, we have to split it into sentences of manageable size in our language, without causing any damage to its original meaning and taking sufficient care that it does not sound odd in the target language. For example, when you translate from English to Malayalam, many sentences, where the relative pronouns, adverbs and prepositions come in between the main clause and the sub-clause, a shift in the position of the sub-clause becomes desirable and sometimes inevitable too. For example:

1. She is asking you where you have come from.
2. I would like to know why you are so silent.

In sentences like these, the shifting of the sub-clauses is inevitable:

1. *Nee eviteninnanu varunnathennu avar chothikkunnu* (Malayalam) *Neenu ellinda bandiddendu avaru keluthiddare* (Kannada)
2. *Nee enthinaanu onnum mintaththathennu enikku ariyanam* (Malayalam) *Neenu yaake summane iddee endu nanage gottu.* (Kannada)

Adverbs like if, though, as, since etc. are found in the beginning of English clauses. But in our regional languages, we have to shift them to the end of the clauses.

1. If he comes now. . . . *Avan ippol vannenkil. . . .* (Malayalam) or *Avanu eega bandare . . .* (Kannada).
2. Since last Monday . . . *Kazhinja Thinkalazha muthal. . . .* (Malayalam) or *Kaleda Somavaaradinda. . . .* (*Kannada*)
3. As I was ill. . . . *Enikku asukhamayathukontu. . . .* (*Malayalam) or Nanage husharilladdarinda. . . .* (Kannada)

To present the sentences in the target language in the most natural way, it does not matter if we use certain new words, which are not found in the original. It is quite alright if your sentence faithfully brings out the essential spirit of the original.

Changes should be made in the use of passive voice and indirect speech in English. They are very common and look very natural there. But if you translate it as it is, it spoils the beauty of translation. For example, if you translate 'It was done by him' as '*athu avanekkontu cheyyappettu*' or '*Macbeth* is written by Shakespeare' as '*Macbeth Shakespearekkontu ezhuthappettu*' (Malayalam) it looks very artificial. Though *Karmani prayogam* is there in our language too, it is used in different a context. Similarly 'He said that he would be going to Delhi' becomes '*Avan Delhiyilekkku pokunnu ennu paranju.*' (Malayalam)

Indian languages have their own system of word order. Subject-verb-object is the word order in English, but, subject-verb-object is the order in our regional language. If you change the order in English, the sentence completely loses its meaning. But in our language, whichever order you put the words in, nothing happens to its meaning. Only that, in the unusual order the sentence looks a little odd. Besides, in English, no sentence can be made without a verb. But it is not so in our language. '*Ithu oru veedanu* (Malayalam) or *Idu ondu mane* (Kannada), *athu oru nagaramanu* (Malayalam) or *Adu ondu nagara* (Kannada) '*njangal vidyarthikalanu*' (Malayalam) *or Naavu vidyarthigalu* (Kannada) are examples. Therefore, when you translate from English, articles and copula verbs need not be translated as they are. For example, 'He was waiting at the bus stop.' *Avan bus stoppil kaththunilkunnuntayirunnu* (Malayalam) *or Avanu bus stoppinalli kayuttidda* (Kannada)

Just like prepositions and articles are used in English, we use *vibhakthi prathyayas* to connect to connect the words in a sentence. We should be careful about the use of these *prathyayas* when we translate from English or to English. Sometimes in English, the same preposition is used with different meanings, for which we have different *prathyayas.*

1. He came by bus: *Avan bassilanu vannathu* (Malayalam) *or Avanu basnalli banda* (*Kannada*)

2. He will finish the class by 4 o' clock: *Avan nalu manikk class theerkum*. (Malayalam) or *Avanu naalku gantege class mugisuttane* (Kannada)
3. He made it by heart. *Avan athu kanaathe parayan pathichu*. (Malayalam) or *Avanu adannu bayipaatha kalitha* (Kannada)
4. It was written by Shelley: *Adu Shelley ezhuthiyathanu* (Malayalam) or *Adannu Shelley barediddaane*. (Kannada)

Certain expressions in all languages are culture specific. Though similarities could be found among different cultures, there are certain elements in every language which give it a separate identity. The translation of such culture specific elements causes problems. Some customs may have positive connotations in some cultures, and some others may consider the same as negative. In such cases the translator has to take his/her freedom to make proper changes in his/her translation carefully so that no harm is done to the intention of the original work.

The problems caused by the personality and character-related matters during translation are called endocentric. That means, it is related to the contribution of the translators as an artist to the artistic beauty of the work.

The translator should be able to surrender his /her full personality to the original writer and achieve a union with him/her. Then only he/she will be able to enter into the mental condition of the original author at the time of the creation of that work. Then only he/she will be able to get across the entire process through which the original writer's imagination has passed through. This enables him/her to follow the same path through which the original writer has walked. In order to achieve this union with the original writer, the translator has to keep his/her personality at suspension. This negative capability on the part of the translator only makes him/her give the replica of the original one. If this does not take place, there will be two kinds of dangers:

1. The translator, though intelligent and talented by himself/herself, fails to rise to the level of the original writer.
2. The translator's personality outshines the personality of the original write. Both these extremities are undesirable.

In the former case, translation is deprived of the spirit, making it ineffective and an 'under translation.' And in the latter, it goes ahead of the original work and becomes an 'over translation.' An ideal translator remains away from both these extremities, and becomes successful by his fidelity to the original work.

The obligation to forge equivalence compels the translator to look very closely at the original, as well as to consider carefully what alternatives he/ she can offer in translation. Thereby the translator is tested twice over. First, he/ she is tested in terms of reception—what he/she makes of the original text. There will be variants of meaning. All these variants, including the wrong ones, should be apparent to the translator, before h/she chooses one which seems to be more suitable in the context. The second test is of the translator's command of the two languages involved, especially where the latter is concerned, in terms of transmission. The greater his/her resource in the latter, the greater are the chances of his/her being able to transmit what he/she has received of the original text. In fact, if the translator of literary works is also a writer himself/herself in his/her target language, with adequate experience of other composition, he/she would be better equipped to transmit than if he/she never wrote at all but only translated.

The simplest test of a good translation is its fidelity and approximation to the original. In the modern text-based translation, the translator's task is much simpler because fidelity to the original must be his/her primary and steadfast aim, making allowances only for the unavoidable lexical or linguistic, cultural or environmental adjustments with the original.

Rather than discussing translation in the context of world literature, it is more imperative that we discuss it in the Indian context. In a multi-lingual country like ours, it is sad to note that the literature of different languages is compartmentalized in such a way that a mutual exchange is possible only through a foreign language. Indian literature continues to be without a common literary forum which could be shared by all Indian languages. It is the experience of those who have attended All India Writers' Conferences or Inter language literary seminars how frustrating it is to hear about notable achievements in another sister language without being able to sample such achievements in any practical way. The literary compartments in which we live in India—with windows wide open to non-Indian literatures, but the doors closed to the work of our own neighbours—tend to grow, rather than diminish in spite of the organized attempts at bringing together writers, critics, and readers from different languages. As an editorial in the now defunct journal *Indian Writing Today* complained: 'Indian writers and critics have generally not taken the trouble to acquaint themselves with the literary achievements in languages other than their own, and therefore discussions at these inter language meets soon become a string of inane generalities. The discussions are, so to say, conducted in a vacuum, and the whole thing becomes an exercise in futility.' This makes it very clear that there is a dire need for the solidarity of Indian Literature through an exchange of literary works among all Indian languages through translation.

Of course, the independent government of India has shown some awareness of this problem by setting up, soon after 1947, a Central Academy of Letters—The Sahitya Akademi at Delhi, whose function is to 'work actively for the development of Indian letters and to set high literary standards, to foster and to co-ordinate literary activities in all Indian languages, and to promote through them all the cultural unity of the country.' In tangible terms, its annual awards publicize the outstanding books of each Indian language; its publications make a particular work in one language available through translation in several other languages. Another such project of the central government is the *Adan-Pradan* program of the National Book Trust. Of late, a large number of private investments in publication have voluntarily come forward for linking Indian languages and literatures. Because of the work taken up by these institutions only, some amount of exchange of literatures has become possible among all Indian languages. Premchand and Mahadevi Varma of Hindi, Sharatchandra Chatterjee, Bhibhoothi Bhooshana Bandopadhyaya and Mahasweta Devi of Bangla, Fakirmohan Senapati of Gujarati, Amrita Pritam, and Bhai Vir Singh of Punjabi, Subrahmanya Bharathi of Tamil, M.T. Vasudevan Nair, S.K. Pottekkat, Thakazhi Sivasankara Pillai, Vaikom Mohammed Basheer, Keshavdev and Uroob of Malayalam, Shivaram Karanth, U.R. Ananthamurthy, Poornachandra Tejaswi, Girish Karnad, D.V.G. D.R. Bendre and Kuvempu of Kannada have become familiar to the Indian readers owing to the translation work undertaken by them. The Central Sahitya Akademi has recently taken up the translation of ancient literature too, which is really a commendable job.

But again, the irony of the situation is that majority of them are ignorant of the original language in which they have been written. Unless English is used as a mediator, translation in India becomes almost impossible. However, a translated work, which comes to a language from an already translated version becomes a doubly filtered one and so 'twice removed from reality.' Hence it loses the essential elements of the original work. Therefore, a direct translation is always preferable to the indirect one. And for this, the governmental institutions which have undertaken the promotion of translation should think of making some arrangements for learning of languages among the Indians, other than their native tongue.

Who is a good translator, and how should he take up his work? If translation is done with some ulterior motive or by monetary inducement or by self-aggrandizement, it will not produce the desirable results. These means may serve functional purposes—as for example, in Parliament reports or advertising copy or radio news bulletins. Translation of literary material seems to demand much more than competence in two languages. Yet, the precise requirement is so elusive that no theory or stated practice of translation has been enunciated or published that seems satisfactory on all accounts. At best we can talk around and about the problem, without aspiring to say anything definitive. As with an original piece of writing beyond a stage, translation work also entails creativity, and is therefore not amenable to the kind of analysis that can lead to emulation.

It is not only for the pleasures of reading or just for the curiosity of learning what is being done in other languages that translation becomes important, but for a greater cause like building up comparative literature at the world level. The different forms of literatures like national literature, world literature and general literature are necessary for streamlining the subjects of comparative literature. In fact, national literature forms the basis of comparative literary order. For the study of comparative literature on a vast scale, a vast and comprehensive knowledge of national literature becomes necessary. Comparative literature at the world level will lead the nations of the world to a perfect understanding of each other, or at least develop a feeling of tolerance for each other. But in the case of India, though the ancient literature had been available in languages known to people in general, the modern literature is available in different languages, not commonly known. For comparative literature at the world level, every nation has to form a single history of literature, which is not possible in a multi-lingual nation like India. From this point of view, for the solidarity of a single Indian literature, translation is the need of the day.

When a literary work is written in its original language, it responds to the Time and Space where it is written. But its translation takes its rebirth keeping in view its own Time and Space, which is different from the original. From this point of view, a literary translation is not the replica or imitation of the original, but it is a creative rebirth.

It does not mean that translation rejects the original. However, despite denial, it gives scope for its creative growth too. It is all relative, depending on the objective of translation. A translation may remain faithful to the original. Based on the original, it may be expanded, collected or recreated. If the objective is to recreate the cultural environment of the original, the ground of the process of translation will be different. For this, the translator will have to learn a lot about the culture of the original. This happens in the case of direct translation. But, if it is done through English, the effect of cultural specifities will be completely lost. Those who do literary translations are in a better position than those who do translations in the field of Science or Media, because in literature they are free to transcreate the original.

Points to be pondered:

- Problems in translation are different from the translators' problem.
- Different types of translations by different translators will be different because all of them interpret the original in their own way. It is like the Re-reading of the myth.
- There are regional variations in the same language. Therefore the need may arise to translate within the language.
- Linguistic or cultural ethos of the original work cannot be translated exactly as it is. Should it retain the linguistic rhythm & Cultural identity or should the translator change them to make his readers feel that it is a creative work? This is to be discussed.
- Translator has to take care of the smallest details.

Works Cited

Gurudat, Pradhan. *Bhashantara Kale.* Bengaluru; Sapna Books, 1989.

Jaware, Aniket. *Simplifications.* Hyderabad; Orient BlackSwan, 2001.

Mukherjee, Sujit. *Translation as Discovery*. Hyderabad: Orient Longman, 2006.

Niranjan, Tejaswini. *Siting Translation.* University of California Press: Paperback, 1992.

Linguistic Structures and Issues of Intercultural Translation: An Overview

Translation is a familiar tradition of long standing, rather than a recent or specialized activity in the literature of every language in the world. And, in a country with so much of linguistic fragmentation like India, for national integration and intercultural relationship, translation has been considered inevitable and an integral part of life. 'Almost every one of the new Indo Aryan languages which emerged between the 10th and 15th centuries, tested its new found prowess at a crucial stage of its development by translating and adapting the *Mahabharata* and the Ramayana. . Since then translation has occupied as natural a place in our literary writing as it has in our every day speech. (Mukherjee, 126)

If you go to the history of translation literature in Kannada, you may observe that the dialectics of inter semiotic relationship had its entry into it in the 10th century itself. Though not in the modern sense, what the poets of those times—Pampa, Ranna, Janna, Harihara, Raghavanka, Kumaravyasa, Nagavarma etc-virtually did was nothing but the translation of the ideas which they got from the Sanskrit texts. The same may be said about the literary works of those times in other regional languages too. The concept of translation transcended from the idea-based translation to the text-based one, only during the 19th century, because of the colonial intervention. Through their intensive and extensive study of language and culture, the western linguists had already evolved the concept of inter-semiotics and text-based translation. The colonial influence changed our definition of translation as changing from one language to another, without changing the meaning or retaining as much of the sense of the original as one can. 'If language is the body and the matter soul, translation is changing the body without damaging the soul.' (Gurudut 8)

The globalization of the world has increased the need for translation more than ever before. The contact among the people of all corners of the world has been made a reality, and hence cultural exchange has become an everyday affair. This has boosted the inter-semiotic relationship through translations among the western and eastern languages, as well as among the Indian regional languages. Thus we may see a boom of translated literature in Kannada also in recent years.

What kind of themes in general do the Kannada readers expect from translations? From what perspective do they read the translated works? What are their interests and preferences? If you just take a cursory glance at the spectrum of translation literature in Kannada, you will understand that the readers' tastes are manifold. They are attuned to themes which are new to them or the familiar themes treated in a new light. They are motivated to read anything that adds a new colour to the already existing literature; they feel thrilled to be introduced to any linguistic structure which widens the horizon of their knowledge and experience of any area which is sparsely cultivated in Kannada. That is why, the literary works in other languages that deal with the dialectics of religious, cultural, political and sociological issues of the time, have been translated into Kannada for which there is a tremendous response from the Kannada readers. Within the limitations of my reading of the translations of the new millennium, I have prepared this paper on the present scenario of Kannada translation literature.

Based on their themes and content I may divide the translation works in Kannada as those which depict:

- Class politics and exploitation of the poor and the downtrodden

- The impact of colonial rule on the Indians
- The works projecting feminist concern
- Novels on the inhuman face of partition politics
- Man's feeling of isolation
- Autobiographies and other prose writings
- Translation of English text presenting a different cultural world.

Class Politics and Exploitation of the Poor and Downtrodden

Here we have the translations of the novels and short stories of writers like Mahasweta Devi, Bhibhuthibhooshana Bandopadhyaya, Premachand, Thakazhi, Basheer, Gopinath Mohanty and several others. We see a very strong sense of social commitment in their works. An anthology of short stories of Mahasweta Devi titled *Bete* in Kannada depicts the agonies, sufferings and exploitation of the tribals. Her novel called *1084ra Thaayi* passes on the message that we should fight against injustice done to the poor in the society. A number of short stories and novels of Thakazhi have come to Kannada in the new millennium, dealing with the exploitation of the Dalits. The short stories and novels of Premachand like *Godaan* and *Rangabhoomi* unravel the heartrending stories of the poor and the cruelty of the feudal lords. Bhibhoothibhooshan Bandopadhyaya's short stories and his novel *Pather Panchali* very touchingly describe the life of the poor, their miseries and sufferings, amidst an affluent society which is indifferent to them. A number of short stories and three novellas of Basheer have been translated into Kannada—*Pathummayude Aadu*, *Nduppuppaakkoranundarnu* and *Premalekhanam.* Basheer's choice of themes, his way of handling them, his light humour, his concern for the poor, his love of nature—seen in all his works have made him an icon in the eyes of the Kannada readers. Besides, Basheer is an ideal example to show how translations can influence another literature. After reading Basheer only some of the Muslim writers in Kannada like Boluvaru Mohammed Kunji, Sara Aboobaker, Phakeer Mohammed Katpadi, Banu Mushtak and many others began to write boldly about the exploitation taking place in the Muslim community in the name of religion and tradition.

The translation of Toppil Mohammed Miran's Tamil novel into Kannada under the name *Kadala Teerada Ondu Gramada Kathe* describes the cruelty and heartlessness of feudalism in a Muslim village where the villagers remain ignorant of what is happening in the outside world. The harsh realities of how the social and religious leaders misuse their power are depicted here in a very moving but dispassionate manner. This novel has been very beautifully translated by Sesanarayan. This is the first novel in Tamil with Muslim sensibility. Another novel which describes the blind beliefs and rigidity of Muslim customs is N.P. Mohammed's *Daivathinte Kannu* translated by Parvati Aital. Sesanarayan has also translated another anthology of short stories by Akhilan, with the title *Tamilu Saurabha*. These stories are woven round the poverty and wretchedness of small children.

The translation of the long-short stories of the Telugu writer, Kalipatnam Ramarao, under the title *Yajna* is a good contribution to Kannada literature. All his stories here have got a strong political undercurrent of the class war. He depicts the cruelty of the capitalists and the feudal lords exploiting the poor labourers and the downtrodden. This book has been published by the Central Sahitya Akademi.

The Impact of Colonial Rule on the Indians

A comparative picture of the life of the Indian villages during the pre-colonial and the post-colonial periods could be seen in some of the literary works translated into Kannada. M. Mukundan's *Daivathinte Vikrithikal* which is titled in Kannada as *Devara Vikaralakalu* (trans. Na. Da. Shetty) is an example. In a very picturesque manner it depicts the life of the people of

Mayyazhi village before the advent of the Portuguese and the changes which took place in them after their departure. The Kannada translation of the Tamil novelist Karlo's *Ivaru katheyadavaru* also gives a similar experience.

Works projecting Feminist Concern

The translation of literary works having serious feminist concern has always drawn a vast readership in Kannada. Parvati G. Aital's translation of *Malayalathinte Pattu Kathakarikal* as *Malayalada Hatthu Kathegarthiyaru* has worked wonders in the Kannada literary world. It is not only a collection of short stories by women writers, but it also presents a detailed interview of the individual writers, eliciting their view of life, literature and the present condition of the society (Editor of its original version is Sridevi K. Nair). This book has won the hearts of the readers and it has been considered an important reference book in libraries for those who pursue their research work on feminism. Besides, being influenced by it, a very similar book compiling the short stories and interviews of the eminent women writers of Kannada was published immediately. Similarly, Sara Joseph's novel *Aalahayude Penmakkal*, translated by Parvati Aital which describes the marginalized and downtrodden women has been received with great zeal. Feminist concern and a deep concern for the protection of environment against man's greed are seen in N.P. Mohammed's *Daivathinte Kannu* also. Prajna Pawar's short stories in Marathi translated by Chandrakant Pokale also are having feminist concern. Himanshu Joshi's Hindi novel *Kagar Ki Aag* (*Antima Jwaale* in Kannada) and the anthology of Ravi Patnayak's short stories called *Vichitra Varna* also are filled with deep feminist concern

Novels on Partition Riots

Novels on partition riots and its horrifying violence are very rare in Dravidian languages. However, this vacuum has been filled by translations. Two such translations have in Kannada—one is Amrita Pritam's *Pinjar* translated by L.C. Sumitra and another, Khushwant Singh's *Train to Pakistan*. Both of them describe how communal prejudice and partition politics led to irreparable human sufferings and loss of innocent lives. Apart from the account of reality they also prove, though in a Utopian fashion, how the bond of human love transcends this blindness and wins ultimately. There is a Malayalam novel too by Unnikrishnan Tiruvayiyod, translated into Kannada almost of a similar theme, under the title, *Indiragandhiya Hathyeye Balika* (trans. K.K. Nair) which deals with the blood-curdling massacre of the Sikhs in Delhi after the murder of Indira Gandhi.

Subjective Themes—Man's feeling of Isolation

Central Sahitya Akademi and National Book Trust are the two governmental institutions that have encouraged translations among regional languages. They are highly selective when they recommend books for translations. Their criteria for selection are: either they should have received Sahitya Akademi Awards or they should be the books written by a major writer. M.T. Vasudevan Nair, Thakazhi, Basheer and Pottekkat's novels had already been translated into Kannada like this. M.T.'s novels *Nalukettu* and *Kalam* translated by B.K. Thimmappa, *Asuravith* and *Manju* which were later translated by Parvati Aital and a large number of short stories translated by K.K. Gangadharan, Mohana Kuntar, C. Raghavan and others—all of which, in one way or other, depict the internal suffering of man being made a victim of the society's cruelty, and his feeling of isolation—which he writes in a very touching manner have mesmerized the Kannada readers. Thus M.T. Vasudevan Nair is as much a Kannada writer as he is in Malayalam. That is why when Karnataka Sahitya Akademi undertook the project of publishing the monographs of some Jnanapith awardees, it chose M.T. Vasudevan Nair also. The translation of Balachandra Nemade's Marathi novel *Kosala* also scrutinizes the gulf between the private life of the individual and the octopus grips of the social system on him.

Autobiographies

A number of autobiographies, giving the realistic picture of the life of famous writers have been translated into Kannada. Apart from presenting a reward of events from their personal experiences they tell about the views of the authors of life, their observation of the world around them and the contemporary society. The popular among them are Baby Thaayi Kambale's autobiography from Marathi, Madhavi Kutty's three autobiographies *My Story*, *Balyakala Smaranangal* and *Neermadala Poothakalam* from Malayalam, *Babi Haaldar's Novu Tumbida Baduku* from Bengali, *The Autobiography of Sex Worker* by Nalini Jameela, because of its sensational theme, has become controversial among the Kannada readers too.

The translation of an autobiography in Tamil, written by a Hijda, about her gender transformation and the traumatic experiences that she has narrated, is the first of its kind in the literary history of India. It has been brought to Kannada by Tamilu Selvi with the title *Naanu Avanalla Avalu.* The book narrates in a very heartrending manner the discrimination made by the society against the hijdas, who suffer for no fault of theirs.

Two great prose epics in Sanskrit have been translated into Kannada for the first time. One is Subandhu's *Vasavadatta* which depicts the cultural world of 5th and 6th centuries. Another is Banabhatta's *Kadambari* which is titled in Kannada as *Pundalika.* Though the same book had been translated twice earlier, this new version has come out with certain changes, keeping in mind the contemporary readers.

Translation of Poetry

The well-known poet in Kannada H.S. Sivaprakash has translated an anthology of Malayalam poems by Sachidanandan.

But here, instead of the spirit of the original Malayalam, the translator's poetic quality stands prominent. Same thing can be told about U.R. Ananthamurthy's translation of Yeats' poems in his collection *Satamanada Kavi Yeats.* However H.S. Sivaprakash's another anthology of poems called *Maru Roopagalu*, he has included poems of various countries and a variety of linguistic structures. These poems hane been chosen, as he himself says in his foreword, for the purpose of overcoming the monotony which the present Kannada poetry is suffering from. That is why he has covered these poems from various cultures, giving them the new robe in Kannada. Here we may remember the first collection of such poems made by the famous poet B.M. Sree in the sixties called *English Geethagalu* that had a tremendous impact on the *Navodaya* Movement in Kannada poetry. Apart from these, a recent translation of *Gitanjali* has come with a lot of changes for better in its style and presentation.

Translations of Omer Khayyam's *Rubait* from Urdu, of the great epic *Silappadikaram* from Tamil and of the Chinese folk songs have opened a new vista of a variety of unknown cultures.

Translation of Plays for Theatre

Theatre in Kannada is fast growing. It is after the seventies, there started a Theatre Movement all over Karnataka with the staging of plays with modern and relevant themes. With the advent of the latest techniques there was a surge of translated version of plays from other languages. There was an awareness among the theatre lovers that the plays to be staged should respond to the need of the hour; that they should answer the questions arising in the contemporary scenario, with an eye on the present day politics, war, violence, cruelty, atrocity, hypocrisy, corruption and hollowness. That is why, apart from staging the plays of Kannada playwrights, it began to translate a number of plays from western languages. Sophocles, Euripides, Shakespeare, Chekov. Ibsen, Moliere, Bernard Shaw, Brecht and

Becket entered Kannada Theatre either through adaptation or through translation. Re-reading of the Indian myths giving them a new interpretation and making them relevant to the contemporary situation also has been done through the translation of Sanskrit drama—texts like those of Kalidasa, Sudraka Bhasa, Bhavabhuti and others. In a way, the plays of the renowned playwrights of Kannada—Girish Karnad, Chandrasekhara Kambar, P. Lankesh, H.S. Sivapraksh are adaptations from myths, legends, folklore and history. They have developed the ideas from those sources to suit their needs.

Translation as a Production for the Masses

In this category, the translations are demanded by the reading public. The quality of the books here depends upon the demand for them in the target language. The literary value of the work is not considered in this context. The question of choice does not trouble the translator here. Such translations are undertaken mainly for magazines, periodicals, and also on demand from certain publishers. A large number of such Telugu novels, mainly Yandamoori's have been pooled into the libraries of Karnataka. Normally these stories are woven round social situations like dowry problem, inter-caste marriage and a superficial picture of how women are ill treated and exploited—all with black and white characters.

Translation of English Works Open a New Cultural World

Translation of several novels from English has extensively widened the horizon of Kannada readers' world view. Mary Shelley's *Frankenstein* (trans. Shyamala Madhava) which talks about the dangers of going against nature by stretching the use of Science beyond limit, Margaret Mitchell's *Gone With the Wind* about the atrocities of war, Pearl S. Buck's *Good Earth* (trans. Parvati Aital) about man's passionate love of the Earth and his deep feeling of attachment for nature, Ngugi Va Thiongo's *Devil on the Cross* (trans. Banjagere Jayaprakash) describing the miseries of people in the postcolonial Kenya, Randy Posh's novel *Last Lectures* (trans. S. Umesh) about the author's feelings when he stands in the face of death, Italo Kalvino's *Kosimo* (trans. K.P. Suresh) which gives the most interesting and the most unusual account of a man who lives throughout his life only on the trees as though mocking at all our progress and civilization and Khushwant Singh's novel *Train to Pakistan* (trans. M.B. Ramamoorti) describing the traumatic experiences of the people of the border region during partition. The experience of reading the translation of these and more such novels has become an open sesame to the Kannada readers.

Most of the translations in Kannada have been done either from original English texts or the English or Hindi version of other regional languages or from original Hindi texts. Very few Kannada works have been taken into other languages, and most of them are to English. Fictional writings of Shivaram Karanth, U.R. Ananthamurthy, Kuvempu, Kambar, S.L. Bhyrappa, the poetry of D.R. Bendre, D.V.G., the plays of Karnad, Kambar, Lankesh, H.S. Shivaprakash are the main among them. A few short stories here and there have been published in Katha series, *Aniketana* published by Karnataka Sahitya Akademi and Indian literature. Karnad's two plays—*Hayavadana* and *Nagamandala*—have been translated into Malayalam by C. Kamaladevi. Payyannoor Kunjiraman has translated an anthology of short stories of Bhanu Mushthak. K.K. Nair has translated Sara Aboobaker's much acclaimed novel in Kannada *Chandragiriya Theeradalli* which gives a graphic picture of the exploitation of women in the Muslim community. Most of the fictional writings of S.L. Bhyrappa have been translated into different other languages. One of the recent translations of Kannada short stories into Malayalam is *Kannada penkathakal* by Parvati Aital. It is an anthology of short stories of 12 women writers, the stories dealing with women.

Conclusion

Though we often talk about national integrity, our ignorance of other languages keeps us away from the people of other states, their literature and culture. Quite ironically, we know English better than the language of our next-door neighbours. The Indian situation is such that direct and mutual translation among Indian regional languages takes place very rarely. Most of the times, it is through English that a work in regional language goes to another regional language. Besides, only the contemporary literature is given preference by many translators when they translate at the individual level. Our rich heritage of ancient literature and folk literature are not considered. This is a very disappointing situation. It is high time we do something for this. Governmental institutions like Central Sahitya Akademi and State Akademies only can take up some projects for organizing some workshops where group work will be done to effectively bring out translations of such valuable literature. Of course, it has started doing this with the translation of the 16th century Kannada poet Sarvajna's poetry into all regional languages as well as English. Such projects should be done repeatedly and regularly. Though not for national integrity, at least to understand the wealth of our multilingualism and multiculturalism, we should go for the study of languages and translation thereby.

Works Cited

Gurudatt, Pradhan. *Bhashanthara Kale.* Bengaluru: Sapna Books, 1989.

Kuntar, Mohan. *Bhashantharada Vibhinna Nelegalu*. Hampi: Kannada University, 2008.

Mukherjee, Sujit. *Translation as Discovery.* Hyderabad: Orient Longman, 2006.

Niranjan, Tejaswini. *Siting Translation*. University of California Press: Paperback, 1992.

Translation Between Kannada and Malayalam Literature

Kannada and Malayalam belong to the South Dravidian group of languages of the two neighbouring states. But they are not as close to each other as Kannada and Tamil or Kannada and Telugu are from the point of view of their structure and script. There is a lot of gap between the two languages culturally also, when compared to Tamil and Telugu which are the two major Dravidian languages. One of the main reasons for this difference is the presence of the Western Ghats which stretch across the North-South direction, as well as the presence of the perennial rivers of the Sahyadri range. Another reason is the political isolation of Kerala from Karnataka mainland for several centuries.

Everyone knows that any language varies in its usage from region to region depending upon its various dialects. A single language also may be having several forms like spoken, written, colloquial, standard, social and so on. Thus there may be a lot of discrepancies and complications in its usage. The people who speak Dravidian languages as their mother tongue in South India have several cultural habits related to their rites, rituals, traditions and customs, though they differ from each other in some of their features, which make them form a separate sub-culture. That is why in Dakshina Kannada district, the people who speak Tulu as their mother tongue—though politically they come under Karnataka state, form a separate sub-culture of their own and differ from the other people of the main land in several aspects.

Despite these differences, we may see a linguistic link between Kannada and Malayalam existing for a long time.

Tulunadu, comprising the present Udupi and Dakshina Kannada districts Kodagu were under the care of Kannada rulers before the advent of the British. Thereafter, when these regions merged with the Madras Presidency, Kannada language continued to be the administrative language and the medium of education, while Malayalam continued to be the language used for the same purpose in the Malabar area. Thus the two languages co-existed in this part of Madras Presidency for some time with mutual give-and-take process, even before the formation of states in India according to the languages spoken in the region.

The oldest reference book which gives details about Malayalam grammar and poetics is *Leelathilakam*. It provides sufficient proofs of its authors being influenced by the Kannada treatises on the same subject. The two sub-cultures also seem to have been influenced by the Christian missionaries who brought out a number of translations. After Independence the cultural contacts between Kerala and Karnataka received a new impetus through the publication of several two-way translations, as a result of which there was a cultural assimilation between the two linguistic groups.

The process of translation between Kannada and Malayalam can be broadly classified under three heads: Phonological level, Lexical level and Syntactic level.

Phonological level: Kannada alphabet consists of 52 letters whereas Malayalam consists of 54 letters. Kannada does not have '*ra*' and '*zha*' which Malayalam has got. Because of this, from the point of view of pronouncing certain Malayalam words, Kannada speaker will face a problem. When you transliterate some Malayalam names of persons or places, you cannot write them in Kannada exactly as they are. Besides, the pronunciation style of Malayalees is different from that of the Kannadigas. The letters *Ka, Cha, Ta, Tha, Pa* when they are used as medial phonemes or at the end of words, the Malayalees use their allophones *Ga, Ja, Da, Dha, Ba*, which practice is not seen among the Kannadigas. For example: *Kanakadhara*, *Mookambika*, *Panchamritham*.

When *Ta* is half-written in Malayalam either as medial phoneme or at the end of a word, it is pronounced as *l*. For example: *Valsalya*, *Malsaram*, *Kaval* etc. The translation into Kannada should be carefully rendered here.

If a translation is undertaken just by listening to the language being read out by someone, without knowing these differences, it will lead to wrong spellings.

Lexical Level: In the process of translation, the choice of appropriate words to convey the message as required by the source language to the readers of the target language is very important. Normally we consult a bilingual dictionary to find a suitable synonym to be used in the target language. However, two things are to be noted here:

1. There are several shades of meanings given to a word in the dictionary. The translator has to pause to see which meaning suits the context most, and select the same.
2. As in all Indian languages, we may find a number of Sanskrit loan words in Kannada as well as Malayalam. However, we must understand that though the same words are used in both the languages, they are used with different meanings and different semiotic contexts. If we do not take sufficient care, we are likely to commit blunders. For example:

    Avakasham in Malayalam means 'Right' but in Kannada it means 'Space' or 'opportunity'

    Avasaram in Malayalam means 'context' but in Kannada it means 'Hurry-burry'

    Bahalam in Malayalam means 'commotion' but in Kannada it means 'Very much'

    Avadhi in Malayalam means 'Holiday' but in Kannada it means 'Period'

There are so many such words in both languages that a small dictionary could be made for it.

Syntactic level: As the structure of sentences in Malayalam varies from those of Kannada in various contexts, word for word translation is not desirable. The copula verb like *aanu* in Malayalam used very often both in spoken and written forms, keeps the two distant from each other in many aspects, as far as the structure is concerned. For example:

1. Malayalam: *Nee enthanu parayunnathu?'* Kannada*: Neenu enu helutthiddi*
2. In conversations between two persons in Malayalam, they do not make use of pronouns but keep repeating the name of the second person. In Kannada, the practice is different. For example:

Malayalam:

Asha: *Usha enne thettiddharikkaruthu.*
Usha: *Pakshe Asha enne pattichchu, alle?*
Asha: *Ushaykku chila karyangal manassilavunnilla.*
Asha:Usha onnum parayanta. Enikku ellam manassilakunnu.

Kannada:

Asha: *Usha, neenu nannannu thappu thiliyabaradu.*
Usha: *Adare Asha, neenu nannannu vanchiside, alva?*
Asha: *Usha, ningae kelavu vishayagalu arthavaguvudilla.*
Usha: Neenu enu helabeda. Nanage ella arthavagatte.

Culture-Specific Words and Expressions

1. In Malayalam *Chetta* means brother. But in the modern society, they have developed a new trend where a woman calls her husband also *Chetta.* But in Kannada, if you translate it as *Anna* (which means 'brother'), it becomes a blunder. So, one should be alert while translating such words.
2. Words like *Tharavadu*, *Nalukettu*, *Karanavar*, *Samabandham*, *Veli*, *Kettukalyanam*, *Thrikkakkarappan*, *olan*, *kalan etc*, are untranslatable, or they lose their essence if they are translated by substituting them with something which resembles them. Therfore it is better if we keep them

as they are by giving their meanings in footnotes. Such culture specific words are there in Kannada too, like the concept of offering *Arasina-kunkuma* to the *Sumangalis*, drawing *Rangoli* designs in front of the houses in the mornings etc. These specific practices should be explained in the footnotes.

3. Though barriers are there between Kannada and Malayalam politically and culturally, they are not found among people living in border regions. The people of border regions like Dakshina Kannada, Kodagu and Mysore districts are bilinguals in their daily affairs. These districts are having direct contact with Kerala through Kasaragod, Kannur and Vyanad districts. Though the two states were divided according to the languages spoken, the people living in these regions have kept cultural relationships with each other, transcending the cultural and political barriers. The give-and-take affairs between the two languages have not remained there as a part of the act of translation. They have become bilinguals or multilinguals quite unconsciously. The people living in the border between Dakshina Kannada and Kasaragod learn a third regional language called Tulu. Similarly, the people of Kodagu and Vyanad districts learn Kodagu language along with their regular Kannada and Malayalam.

In the works translated from Malayalam into Kannada, we may observe mainly three attitudes. They have come into Kannada for three reasons. These are: Function Oriented Applied Translation; The Translations rendered by the Amateur writers; Pedagogic translations.

Function-Oriented Translation: These are the works translated with the purpose of supporting certain activities. The translations rendered on this ground have a particular class of readers, audience, consumers, political organizations and communities as their aim. The works translated from Malayalam into Kannada in this context include *Yakshagana* episodes, medical volumes, political people's autobiography, the thoughts of the social reformers like Sri Narayana Guru and the popular literature translated for the purpose of entertainment. The first important document of the function oriented translation was the Yakshagana episodes of Ramayana by Parthisubba. It has been already identified by scholars as the direct translation of the Ramayana episodes written by the Duke of Kottarakkara. The *Kathakali* episodes written by the Duke of Kottarakkara were significant from the cultural perspective. These *Kathakali* episodes were very popular in Kerala already. When Parthisubba of Kumbla, a Kannadiga by birth, visited the southern part of Kerala, he was very much impressed by these shows and he translated those verses into Kannada with the purpose of experimenting them in *Yakshagana* performed by the Kannadigas. Consequently, Parthisubba was recognized as the exponent of a different variety of *Yakshagana* called *Tenkutittu*. He is very relevant today not only as the one who has refined and polished the *Yakshagana* form, but also as an episode maker. Parthisubba wrote these episodes in the latter half of the 18th century. Prior to this, seen from the theatrical and literary perspective, *Yakshagana* episodes were not available. Parthisubba's Ramayana episodes are valued in the *Yakshagana* field even today. They have become very popular. Thus Parthisubba rendered the translation in order to fulfil the needs of the *Yakshagana* lovers. The episodes which were written later have been obviously influenced by Parthisubba's translations. This is significant from the cultural perspective.

Another important Malayalam work translated into Kannada is *Srithoovennilava.* This is a volume which prescribes medicine for poison. It was published in 1895 under the title *Vishabda Marutha*. It has been translated by Ganesh Saantayya Karebaylekar, for the public well-being. It is in the poetic form. However, the poetic part has been just transliterated. Explaining the subject matter in Kannada was the main objective here. The names of the original writer or the translator or the form of the work have remained unknown. The aim of translation here was giving that knowledge to the Kannada readers. But the fact that its 2000 copies were printed as the first impression itself speaks about its popularity.

Similarly, the Kannada readers' curiosity was roused towards the leftist political thoughts of Srinarayana Guru through the translation of his preachings. People particularly interested in politics and particular communities looked at them with special interest. From this point of view, the translation of E.M.S. Namboothirippad's autobiography *Nanna Baduku* in Kannada and the biography of Srinarayanguru become significant. *Thiruvanthapuram Karnataka Sangham* has published the translations of a few selected Malayalam works of all genres for the purpose of making the Kannadigas settled in Kerala learn about Malayalam literature.

If we observe the translated literary works of Malayalam published in Kannada magazines and periodicals we may understand the enthusiasm of the Kannada readers to read Malayalam literature. In 1988, the Malayalam daily *Latest* organized a workshop at Kasaragod for the translation of Malayalam short stories into Kannada. The stories translated in the workshop were published later by the famous Kannada weekly *Taranga* in its special issue. The same weekly reminded of the Centenary of Malayalam short stories by publishing special issues. The magazines and periodicals in Kannada fulfil the desires of the readers for Malayalam stories by publishing them again and again. And it is to be noted that these stories are of the famous writers only. The *Mangala* weekly has introduced a number of popular writers to Kannada by serializing popular novels. Some decades ago, a monthly called *Prapancha*, edited and published by the great Kannada writer Srikrishna Alanahalli had given special encouragement to the translation of Malayalam literary works. He had brought a special issue on Vaikom Mohammed Basheer too. But all these publications are limited to the temporary fulfillment of the readers' interests because none of them was brought out in book form.

Thus the aim of function oriented translation is fulfilling the contextual needs of the people. Here, the aim of reaching the people through media becomes important. Sometimes, the responsibility of taking them to a particular category of readers is taken up by certain organizations, communities and religious groups too.

Translations Rendered by Amateur Writers: These translations are done by individual writers. On reading a text in the source language, they are inspired to provide it to their readers in the target language. They aim at doing it with all sincerity in the most meaningful manner. Only when they feel that it has been rendered meaningfully, they get it published. Most of them are translations of literary works. Here the translators are familiar with the language and culture of both the languages. The writers who are living or are the natives of the border regions have done a lot in this field. If the form, content, beauty, theme and the style of the narrative impress the translator, he/she sets out on the venture. The first novel was translated from Malayalam to Kannada in 1899. It was Joseph Muliyil's *Sukumari* translated by H. Robert. T. Ubaid, C. Raghavan, K.K. Nair, Karunakaran K.S., M.S. Lakshmanachar, Rama K., Sara Aboobaker, B.K. Thimmappa, K.K. Gangadharan, Ashok Kumar, Na.Da. Shetty, Parvati Aital, Mohan Kuntar, Kamalaksha K., Meenakshi Ramachandran, Ratnakar Mallamoole, Prabhakaran, Suneeta K. and others joined the group later. It is to be noted here that many of them have kept their translations unpublished too. All these have, by constantly trying to bring poetry, novels, short stories and plays from Malayalam to Kannada, made the major Malayalam writers familiar with the Kannada readers. They have not only tried to render them in Kannada, but with their persistent efforts pursued the publishers to print and publish them. The work, the detailed profile of the original author and the supplementary notes for the better understanding of the cultural specifications are collected by them for the purpose of introducing the Malayalam world to the Kannadigas. Since the publishers always grumble about the sales in the Kannada market being poor, and hesitate to publish the translations of even those of the great Malayalam writers, the translators forego the royalty for their efforts (except two or three publishers who pay royalty promptly) and struggle to give them to the Kannada readers. Poetry like *Chinthavishtayaya Seetha*, *Jnanapanam*, *Vaazhakkula*, anthologies of short stories like *Yugantha mattu Ithara Kathegalu*, *Vasudevan Nair Kathegalu*, novels like *Agnisaakshi*, *Asuravitthu*, *Thottiyude Magan*, *Manju*, *Alaahyude Penmakkal*, *Varanasi* and several others could be cited as examples here.

Pedagogic Translations: The universities, Sahitya Akademi, National Book Trust, Translation Akademi, South Indian Language Institute have done a commendable job in getting books of academic importance translated from Malayalam into Kannada.

The universities have got the works of other languages translated and have prescribed them as text books for various courses. When they do this, they select only the works which come within the suitability of their syllabi. Thus Karnataka University has published *Tullal Kathagal*, Bangalore University has published *Kerala Panineeyam*, and Mysore University has published *Leela Tilakam*.

Through the translation project of Sahitya Akademi, the award winning books of Malayalam literature have been translated by the experts in the field. Thakazhi's *Chemmeen* and *Kayar*, M.T. Vasudevan Nair's *Kaalam*, S.K. Pottekkat's *Oru Deshaththinde Katha*, Basheer's *Enduppuppakkoranundarnu*, M. Mukundan's *Daivathinde Vikrithigal*, N.P. Mohammed's *Daivathinde Kannu*, Uroob's *Sundariyarum Sundaranmarum*, Sethu's *Adayalangal*, Sukumara Azhikkode's *Tatvamasi* are the major works. National Book Trust also has undertaken translation projects and has published Basheer's *Pathummayude Adu*, *Balyakalasakhi*, M.T. Vasudevan Nair's *Nalukettu*, Parappuruth's *Aranazhikaneram*, Chandu Menon's *Indulekha*, Thakazhi's *Enippadigal*, Keshvadev's *Kannadi* and Pottekkat's *Vishakanyaka*.

In the cultural and literary context of Kerala, Basheer's name stands very high. He was the first Muslim writer to write satirically on Muslim community. Many stories of Basheer have been translated into Kannada. His novellas had already come in Kannada in the 70s itself. These novellas, though with light humour, depicted the absurd customs, conventions and superstitions found in the Muslim community. An important development to be noted here is how after the publication of these translations of Basheer's stories, Muslim writers in Kannada also started writing stories carrying similar sensibility. And, after the Sahitya Akademi and National book Trust brought out Basheer's translations, a number of amateur writers began to translate Basheer's short stories. The Kannada readers have always welcomed the works of M.T. Vasudevan Nair, S.K. Pottekkat, Thakazhi Sivasankara Pillai and others. Consequently, in the academic field also comparative studies have been undertaken. These translations have made the Kannada readers turn their curious eyes towards Malayalam literature.

The Kannada University in Hampi has organized Kannada-Malayalam poetry translation workshops twice—once in 1996 and another time in 2007 in collaboration with the Central Sahitya Akademi. The poets of both the languages were invited to discuss and exchange their stories and poems. The objective of the workshop was to experiment and see the possibility of translation without the help of English. And, it was proved to be successful. These poems and stories translated in the workshop were published later by the Akademi.

The Institute of Southern Languages, Kannada Sahitya Parishad, Department of Kannada and Culture etc. also have conducted workshops and have got the Malayalam works translated into Kannada. B.K. Timmappa, C. Raghavan, Na.Da. Shetty, Mohana Kuntar, Puninchithaya, Na. Kasturi, Sriksrishna Arthikaje, Parvati Aital, K.K. Nair, K.K. Gangadharan, Ashok Kumar are the major translators to be remembered here. But some of the works translated here were chosen by the institutional authorities, and since the translators did not have the right to choose, the translation has been done rather mechanically. Some of them are translated from their English versions. The selection for translation was made on the basis of their receiving awards. But they were published after a long gap of receiving awards, when the themes of those works lost their relevance. These are the shortcomings of pedagogic translations.

Translations from Kannada to Malayalam also have come large in number. C. Raghavan, K.K. Nair, Kumaran Master, Payyannur Kunhiraman, K. Rama, Ubaidulla, C. Kamaladevi, Sudhakara Ramanthali are the major translators. Shivaram Karanth's *Chomana Dudi*, *Mookajjiya Kanasugalu* and *Sarasamman Samaadhi*, U.R. Ananthamurthy's *Samskara*, *Bharatheepura* and *Avasthe*, Srikrishna Alanahalli's *Kaadu* and *Bhujangayyana Dashavatharagalu*, Chandrashekhara Kambar's *Singarevva mattu Aramane* and *Shikharasoorya*, Sara Aboobekar's *Chandragiriya Theeradalli*, the short stories of Poornachandra Thejaswi and Vaidehi, Niranjan's *Chirasmarana*, Girish Karnad's *Hayavadana* and *Nagamandala*—thus the list runs long. The Kannada women writers' short stories have been brought in an anthology titled *Kannada Penkathakal* by Parvati Aital. In 2011 the Central Sahitya Akademi conducted a workshop in Bangalore for translating the 16th century Kannada poet Sarvajna's *vachanas* into Malayalam. 972 *vachanas* were translated by a group of 6 translators. *Basava Samiti* of Bangalore organized another workshop in Thiruvananthapuram for translating the 12th century Kannada *vachanas* of Basavanna, Allama,

Chennabasavanna, and other famous Vachana poets. The printing and publishing of these *vachanas* are still under process.

It is indeed heartening to think of these attempts made by different organizations. But at the same time it is sad to note that the number of translators between Kannada and Malayalam is coming down due to the demise of some of the senior translators. The young people are not showing much interest in learning a new language other than what they have learnt at school and college. New entries to the translation field seem to be almost nil. It is high time the government gets into some action to make the youngsters to learn another regional language and form a new line of translators.

Works Cited

Gurudat, Pradhan. *Bhashantara Kale*. Bengaluru: Sapna Books, 1989

Kuntar, Mohan. *Bhashantarada Vibhinna Nelegalu*. Hampi: Kannada University, 2008

Mukherjee, Sujit. *Translation as Discovery*. Hyderabad: Orient Longman, 2006

Niranjan, Tejaswini. *Siting Translation*. University of California Press: Paperback, 1992.

The Conflict between Nature and Culture in *Aalahayude Penmakkal* (Aalaha's Daughters)

All cultures recognize and make a distinction between human society and natural world. Culture attempts to control and transcend nature, to use it for its own purposes. Culture is therefore superior to the natural world and seeks to mark or socialize our nature, in order to regulate and maintain relations between society, and the forces and conditions of the environment. Women are identified or symbolically associated with nature, while men are associated with culture. Since culture seeks to control and transcend nature, it is natural that women, by nature of their close association with nature, should also be controlled and contained. (*Women, Culture and Society* 67)

Female subordination, which is universal, is not inherent in the biological differences between the sexes; it is a pan-cultural construct. With the inception and growth of feminism, women wanted to escape from this exploitation by disrupting the entire order of dominant values—economic, social, moral and sexual. They called into question all existing theories, all thoughts, and all languages in as much as these are monopolized by men and men alone. They challenged the very foundations of our social and cultural order, whose organization has been prescribed by the patriarchal system. This could be vividly found in the literary works of several feminist writers. Sara Joseph, an eminent Malayalam writer, staunchly committed to feminism, has made an attempt to refute the superiority of culture over nature in her much acclaimed novel *Aalahayude Penmakkal*, which has won the Sahitya Akademi Award of 2007.

In this novel Sara Joseph delves deep into the roots of a marginalized class that has been lost in the sound and fury of culture and civilization, and she gives a new voice to the essence of their language. She refers to the folk custom of prayer called *Aalahayude Namaskaram* which was believed to drive away the evil spirits. She does it mainly with the purpose of showing the power of nature and women. So it has got metaphorical connotations.

All the events in the novel take place in the consciousness of an eight year old girl called Annie, who is virtually the narrator of the story herself. Just like Wordsworth's Lucy Gray, Annie is innocent and immaculate, and could be taken as a part of nature. Her observations have been recorded in the most objective and dispassionate tone in the novel. She is always puzzled by the ways of the world. It is a world of men and men alone. All customs, conventions and beliefs are designed according to the wish and wll of men, and women are expected to meekly follow the rules set by men for them. This injustice towards women escapes the eyes of the innocent girl. But the reader does not fail to notice it.

Annie's grandmother Mariam is the central character in the novel. She has learnt those mysterious incantations from her own grandmother, who had passed it on to her ears from her deathbed. Annie also is very anxious to learn it. She has great fascination for her grandmother's power to relieve the 'possessed' children, whenever the women folk approached her with such complaints. However, Annie's mother strongly disapproves of it because, according to her, it is trespassing and irreligious:

> One should not intrude into the authority of the priests. Should not go to test God. Because of disobedience to God only, one son has left and another taken to bed in this house. Is there any happiness to those who have been given in marriage? Can't anyone see the two unmarried daughters groaning here? (10)

Annie's mother has come from a family of believers. That is why her mother-in-law's practice disgusts her. Verbal battles constantly take place in the house for the same reason.

Earlier, all of them in the house were Roman Catholics. But during the time of Annie's aunt Cherichi's marriage, her husband made an agreement with them that all of them be converted as *Syrians*. However, those who were converted ultimately were Cherichi and grandmother only. After this conversion only the daughter-in-law had begun to have a daily quarrel with her mother-in-law, because she thought that all the problems in the house were due to this conversion. The Romans and the Syrians do not go with each other. They will never be:

> Annie is worried about these last words. If the Romans and the Syrians do not go with each other, mother and grandmother would keep quarrelling everyday. The Romans and the Syrians are two churches that will not go with each other. Are these two different Gods just like mother and grandmother are different? And do they keep quarrelling everyday? They say that it did not start today or yesterday, and it was like that right from the day of crucifixion. (12)

The birth of various religions and creeds leading to bigotry is the sign of development of human culture. All the new religions preach about artificial methods of praying to God. Annie's grandmother is closer to nature, and that is why she laughs at the rosary used by the Roman Catholics. Annie's father Kochappan, who has already left home, does not believe in God. Annie's mother is displeased about him in this regard. But Annie's grandmother believes in the original goodness of man: 'Why God? My Kochappan is a good man,' she says. (13)

Mariam has got two sons and five daughters. The elder son Kochappan has left home, no one knows where, leaving his wife with the 19-day-old baby Annie. The second son Kuttippappan is a T.B. patient, bedridden and invalid. The eldest daughter Kunjila is a young widow. She had been given in marriage to a rich man, without knowing about his illness. Hardly a week after their marriage when he died, she was forced to come back to her mother's house. She loses her faith in God and religion, and stops going to church. The compounder Kunjan of Kokkanchara takes pity on her and helps her by giving practical training to her as midwife. Both of them go out together to attend delivery cases. This brings them nearer and they fall in love with each other. However, Kunjan is a married man and his wife Kochumary keeps nagging him everyday on hearing about their relationship.

Mariam's second daughter is Nonu. She marries Kochurodu's (Annie's mother) brother Lasarachan, a priest. As his sister has been deserted by her husband, he takes revenge on Nonu by beating her everyday. At the end of the novel, Nonu runs away with a boy of the neighbourhood. The third daughter of Mariam is the pretty girl Cherichi. An educated and refined man, who is a priest, marries her and takes her away with him to the city. But he does not allow her to keep any contact with her mother's family. Education has not taught him to understand the natural desires of a woman to see her people. The fourth and fifth daughters are Chiyyamma and Chinnamma respectively. When the novel begins they are not married. They work in a button company.

The institution of marriage, with all its corruption and exploitation of women has been strongly attacked in the novel. The pathetic condition of all the marriages in the family resulting in failure and misery leaves us with the question whether, for the natural union of man and woman, marriage is necessary at all. In the world today, marriage has been commercialized to such an extent that man's attitude towards the girl whom he is going to marry is that of a consumer. He and his people test the girl as though she is a product. It happens in the case of Chiyyamma in the novel. At first, two aged men and aged women come to 'inspect' the girl:

> 'Huh. Now you walk a few steps before us. Let us see whether your legs are in good condition or not.' A priest uncle having only his front teeth said. Poor Chiyyamma walked. This end to that end and that end to this.
>
> 'Her hair . . . is it real or artificial?' the old woman asked. Mother loosened the knot and showed Chiyyamma's hair. The old woman put her finger on her nose.
>
> 'Oh! To wet this hair we might need several measures of oil!'
>
> Annie saw her mother's face turning pale.
>
> 'now sing the song' O mother how kind you are.' Let us see whether the girl has any lisping or stammering.' Chiyyamma sang. The three did not have any more questions to ask.' (86)

The customs and conventions designed by men have completely controlled and curbed the natural freedom of women in the society. They are mere puppets in the hands of the patriarchal belief and traditions. The woman does not have the fundamental freedom to speak openly about the parts of her own body. The stigma of immorality will be stuck on her if she utters certain words:

> Commenting on Annie's short hair, the grandmother says, 'After being born as a girl, one should have her head and breast alright, understand?'
>
> Annie's hands moved inside her gown down to her chest. No, 'it' has not come. Chiyyamma and Chinnamma have been telling that it is time to come. When is it going to come? 'Head and breasts' mean what? That too, only if you are born as a girl! Let it be that men need not have breasts. But, don't they need a head? It is possible to ask someone about this, because, pronouncing the word 'breast' is prohibited! Breast! What a word! Pooh! Not at all nice. Can't utter it aloud. (19-20)

The civilized society always looks down upon natural man-woman relationship by calling it immoral. On one occasion in the novel Annie thinks about love. Chinnamma had told her that Kochumary was angry with her husband Kunjan compounder as he was in love with Kunjila. Annie's thoughts run like this:

> If Kunjan compounder loves my aunt, im what way is it a loss to Kochumary? Chinnamma says that it is not right. Kunjan compounder is entitled to love only Kochumary. After marriage, the husband has to love only his wife, and the wife has to love only her husband. It sounded strange to Annie. If a married man falls in love with another woman, what should he do? Except Kochumary, shouldn't Kunjan compounder love anyone else? This is not right. At first, people say that all should love each other. Then they change it and say that the husband has to love only his wife and the wife her husband, if someone tells Annie that she should love only one, she would definitely die. One should not be miserly in love. She has always believed that loving others is something good. (96)

Kunjan compounder and Kunjila become very popular in the village through their successful handling of delivery cases. But once, as ill luck would have it, they come across a very complicated case and they send the patient to the nearby government hospital. The government doctor, jealous and spiteful, snubs them in the public and accuses them of doing illegal medical practice. Unable to bear with this insult, Kunjan commits suicide. But Kunjila faces life boldly.

Mariamma's youngest daughter Chinnamma faces a different kind of problem. The author refers to it quite tactfully. Nature stands against culture in a conspicuous manner here. Annie is a witness to the whole thing, even though she does not understand the head or tail of it. Chinnamma always talks to Annie very intimately. One midnight Annie hears someone crying loudly in some part of her house. When she opens her eyes, neither her granny nor her mother, nor Chinnamma are found in their beds. Annie fumbles in darkness and sails to the place from where the sound was coming. To her great shock, she finds Chinnamma being laid down flat on the ground in the shed. All the others are standing around her. Her mouth has been pressed hard to prevent her sound being heard. She has clothes only on the upper portion of her body. The lower portion is bleeding profusely. Annie is horrified to see the blood. She fears that they are killing her. Terribly frightened by the whole affair, she hurries back to her bed. But her fear turns out to be wrong because, the following morning when she opens her eyes, she finds Chinnamma lying by her side, covering herself up to her neck.

The author does not give an account of the circumstances under which these gory events take place. But she gives a touching description of how the most natural phenomenon like a woman becoming a mother is looked down upon by the civilized society, and how it relentlessly applies its diabolic means to wipe out the creative power of a woman if she went against the norms set by it.

The novel projects the grandmother Mariam as a lively, strong and down-to-earth character. She never cares for others if she thinks what she is doing is right. She exercises her knowledge and skill of performing the rites of' *Aalahayude Namaskaram*, to drive away the evil spirits which trouble the village folk, and she does this much against the protest of her daughter-in-law, who always keeps reminding her that she is trespassing. The incident of the grandmother's sailing to *Tankamani Kettam* with Annie for collecting some rice for her sick son is a vivid proof of her extraordinary courage.

It was the time of famine in the village. Rice was not available anywhere except in the big house at Tankamani Kettam. People used to go there to beg for rice. However, it was not an easy job. Those who wanted to get some rice, should go there with Kochatti. Mariam managed to convince him somehow, and took him with her at midnight, so that the checkpost people might not catch hold of them. It was a desolate and deserted path. They had to walk through the wood in the dark. Kochatti fancied some figure at a distance and expressed his fear of ghosts and goblins. But Mariam did not care. She simply challenged: "Who is that vagabond? Come forward if you have got guts!

Here is Maria of Kokkanchara, do you understand? If you frighten my child, I shall send you to the right place." (74)

At last they reach that big house. A man appeared at the door and asked her whether she had brought the sack. But the granny's answer amazes us. She says that she needs only two fistfuls of rice to give her sick son. Unlike the so-called cultured people who greedily grab things for hoarding for tomorrow, Mariam is satisfied with the little which she actually needs for the present! And, that too, not for herself!

At the end of the novel, as if to punish all those who do injustice and exploitation, nature lets loose her wrath. There is incessant downpour, thunder and lightning for four days, and the whole village is flooded with water everywhere. Mariam's house is located at the heights of the *Gosai Hill.* The flood water reaches up to the level of its bottom. All of them wait anxiously for the rain to stop. The grandmother must have come to know that her last moment has come. That is why she calls Annie near to her, presses her hot lips to Annie's ears and passes on the mysterious incantations to her. She remembers the unfulfilled pledge made by her to the deity of *Ollur* that she would kneel before him carrying Kuttipappan on her back if he got well. Immediately she tells her daughter-in-law to put him on her back. Carrying him like that she climbs up the steps on her knees, praying. For the time she forgets that she is a Syrian, not a Roman Catholic. Both the mother-in-law and the daughter-in-law pray together, forgetting their differences. The rain stops and the rainbow appears. Kuttipappan dies, leaving his T.B. with Annie, who begins to vomit blood. The struggle between nature and culture continues further, as the ending of the novel indicates.

Eco-feminism is another major concern of the novel. The author's protest against the cruelty of man in destroying the natural resources for his selfish ends as well the modern civilization snatching away the naturally acquired freedom of women has been well reflected in the novel. *Kokkanchara* is a backward village in the eyes of the so-called civilized people. With the advent of modern civilization into the village through the Christian missionaries, a school is opened there. They start the construction of a three-storeyed edifice for this purpose. Towards the end of the novel, the terrible assault made on nature for the school building and road construction has been described in a very moving manner.

A tar road is being constructed using a 'stone machine.' It passes through Annie's house causing a lot of damage to their bean-tendrils. Annie used to love its green shining leaves and dappled flowers. It used to shine like a flower-pandal in front of their house:

> It was on the day when the stone machine came that each and every part of the bean-trellis was cut off and thrown away because it obstructed the passing of the machine. Annie was standing there fanning Kuttipappan. When a part of the bean trellis fell down suddenly, the hot sunlight rushed into the house. Kuttipappan closed his eyes. The bean leaves and flowers were crushed under the giant wheels of the stone machine. The machine moved forward with the paste of flowers stuck all over its wheels. Annie began to feel that her own feet were being caught under the wheels (130)

The depiction of the side effects of globalization also gets a place in the novel. The nuns have purchased the large site of *Konni Mestri* (Mestri means mason) for their school building. However, that school is not meant for the poor children of Kokkanchara, but the 'red, plumpy children' of the rich, city people who wear different colour dresses every day. For their sake new roads are constructed in the village, causing a lot of inconvenience and disturbance to the poor people. The soft, red mud roads are converted into tar roads. Annie feels impatient when she sees this:

> Why are all the ways hardened with black stones crushed and fixed on them? Annie realized the beauty of the red mud roads when she

> walked on the tar road. She had got very much upset when she saw the big ditch on the left side of the first curving of the harlot street being filled up and leveled with stones and soil. She silently came home and lay down on the pyol. Whenever she walked that way, the wide ditch standing distinctly used to make her happy. The ditch had been lying there from a long time—as long as her memory went, as long as the memories of her mother, grandmother and all others went; it had been there for crores of years. Now both sides of the harlot street are filled with crushed stone heaps, tar drums, burning ovens, half burnt firewood pieces and working tools scattered everywhere. There is no space even to put your foot . . . she got very angry. She felt that this is terrible injustice (131)

All the women in the novel, in some way or other bear the characteristic traits of nature in them. Though they suffer a lot, they never accept defeat. They never escape from responsibilities unlike Kochappan, and they never depend upon others unlike Kuttipappan. They do not commit suicide unlike Kunjan compound. All of them stand together at the time of adversity. *Alaaha* is a metaphor which stands for the impeccable courage, immaculate purity and innocence of nature. In a way the old woman Mariam, with all her special skills, herself is *Alaaha* who does not like any evil standing before her. Herself and her daughters face a lot of difficulties and life becomes a constant struggle for them. But their undaunted courage helps them take things positively and cross the hurdles with an unflinching spirit.

The Postcolonial Attitudes of Resistance in M. Mukundan's *Daivattinde Vikritigal* (The Mischiefs of God)

To critically analyze the relationship between the colonizer and the colonized from the earliest days of exploration and colonization—that is what a post-colonial novel does in its course. It focuses on the cultural displacements that inevitably followed the colonial conquest and rule; and it studies the process and effects of cultural displacement along with the ways in which the displaced have culturally defended themselves. It is attentive to the post of colonial attitudes of resistance on the part of the colonized and it seeks to understand the nature of the encounter between the colonizer and the colonized. This colonial discourse is evidently present in M. Mukundan's much acclaimed Malayalam novel *Daivathinde Vikrithikal* (The Mischiefs of God)

The cultural displacement in the life of the poor people of Mayyazhi during the colonial period and after the departure of the French colonizers comprises the central theme of the novel. Depicting the rise and fall in the lives of the people, their beliefs and attitudes, hopes and despair—is the author's major concern here.

A large majority of the people of Mayyazhi belong to a community called *Billavas* or *Teeyas*. Their main occupation is lifting toddy from the palm trees. Their tribe worships the deity called *Adi Billava* for whom they have built a shrine. Mayyazhi is a village where the people lead a contented life. However, after the advent of the Whites, there was a sea change in their way of life. The Whites claim themselves to be civilized and progressive. The people of Mayyazhi become more and more materialistic, being influenced by the Whites. The Whites develop conjugal relationships with the black women and consequently it gives rise to the birth of Anglo-Indians. As the number of fair skins thus increases in Mayyazhi, The blacks begin to develop a feeling of inferiority. Thus the novel throws light on how colonialism affects the life of the common people, and how they try to discard the Whites, and embrace their own culture once again after the colonizers leave the place.

The main character which appears before us as the novel opens is Aphonsacchan (*acchan* means a priest), who is an Anglo Indian. His wife is Maggie, son Michael and daughter Elsie. When the Whites were here, he used to mint money through his magic shows. But today, no one in Mayyazhi cares for magic, and hence he finds it difficult to make both ends meet. Beside, the natives of Mayyazhi hate his brown hair. Alphonsacchan, who had once led a royal life, has to find his happiness only in the world of illusion, created under the effect of poppy. But he is an affectionate and kind hearted soul, and has great love for children. Whenever he sees them on his way, he picks a handful of small stones from the ground and converts them into toffees though his spell and presents them to children. But Maggie has great contempt for her husband as he knows no other work except his magic. She is after money. She wants to live a life of luxury just like the Whites. Her lust for wealth itself instigates her to develop an illicit relationship with Dharmapalan, who had been to France once and has now settled in Mayyazhi as a wealthy man.

Another important character in the novel is Kumaran *Vaidyar* (doctor). The doctor's profession is what he has inherited from his family. Earlier, his father Kunjikutty Vaidyar had been the only doctor in Mayyazhi. Besides, he was also a freedom fighter. When Gandhiji had visited Mayyazhi once,

Kunjikutty Vaidyar had touched his hand just for the thrill of it. But today, the natives of Mayyazhi have lost their faith in the native medicines due to their strong faith in the medicine of the Whites. Even for common cold and indigestion, they go to doctors who have received their degrees from France. Consequently, Kumaran Vaidyar also is suffering from poverty. Besides, his dearest wife Kamala has been dead after delivering the twin boys Sasi and Sivan. Though it was difficult to look after the two small babies single-handed, Kumaran Vaidyar does not marry again because of his sentiments for Kamala. His over-sentimentality for Kamala is just another form of Alphonsacchhan's living in the illusionary world. His hiding behind the ideals of love for his wife and denying a healthy family environment for his children is nothing but escapism. Perhaps, the irresponsible attitude of these two families itself leads to the tragedy of their children later. The small and innocent girl Elsie taking an oath standing before Adibillava that she would marry both Sasi and Sivan, and, without the knowledge of sex, permitting Sasi to have sexual intercourse with her, Elsie becoming pregnant at the premature age of thirteen, her losing interest in life and getting depressed after secretly aborting her foetus, Sasi running away being unable to show his face to any one in Mayyazhi—all these disasters take place only because of the inattentiveness of their parents. However, we cannot forget that the reason for their carelessness is their poverty, which is again due to the change in their way of life after the Whites leave Mayyazhi.

Arupure Kadunga is like the chieftain of the tribe. He is a staunch devotee of Adibillava. He has always stood against the Whites, and has done his best to retain the native culture, faith and tradition. He was born in a respectable family. But his blood relation Kunjaama Vakkil was entirely different from him. His attitude towards the Whites was slavish. Being an advocate, he has contact with most of the Whites and the Anglo-Indians. He was very proud of his position as a friend of the Whites, and he looked down upon the natives. But now, after the departure of the whites, he also has begun to feel like a fish out of water. However, the successive generations of these two, move against the principles of their parents. Rahul, Kadunga's son, gets attracted towards the Whites, and Kunjaama's two sons, whom he forcibly takes to France, return to Mayyazhi, quite against their father's wishes.

The contradiction between the attitudes of Kadunga and Kunjaama has been shown in the beginning of the novel with a subtle humour and irony. Kadunga, even though he hates the Whites, feels inferior about his black colour. His first wife Cheeru was fair-skinned. But, as she used to be always possessed, he abandons her and marries the black-skinned Chappile.

Chappile was so dark that she could never be seen after the lamp was put out—says the narrator. There is humour, as well as Kadunga's despair in this statement. At the same time, Kunjaama feels proud of his fair-complexioned wife.

There is a section of common people who stand apart from all the above said, the so-called established category. They are the poor class, neglected and exploited by the Whites as well as the upper class. The midwife Kunjiruthe, Chattu who used to look after the goats, the umbrella repairer Choyiettan, Rama the saloon, Assanare of the grocery-seller—all these fall under the same category. They are all laborers and hard workers, who used to starve, having nothing to eat, and no money to buy rice. But their succeeding generations go to France or Gulf countries, earn pots of money through their back-breaking work, come back to Mayyazhi and change the face of it by building bungalows there. Kunjiruthe's son Madhavan, Karuthakannan's son Phalgunan, Chattu's son Dharmapalan, Assanare's son Moosa—all these bring about a thorough change in the lifestyle of their elders.

Some of these dalits are influenced by Communism and become revolutionaries. The hot-blooded young man Madhavan, who tries to protest against the Whites, attempts to kill an Anglo Indian called Kommissar, and is chased by the police. Seeing his desperate condition, Kumaran Vaidyar gives him shelter. But, for doing that, he himself had been sent to jail once. The irony of the situation is that Kumaran's son Sivan himself becomes a revolutionary at a later stage, and he stabs Kodunga to death. As the police go in search of him, Madhavan gives him shelter and arranges to send him to Dubai. But, for Sivan, his ideals are more important than money, and therefore he leaves Madhavan's house and runs away.

Alphonsacchan's condition also becomes pathetic. His elder daughter Marie had run away long ago with a police constable. His son Michael, though earns a lot of money in France, falls into bad habits, and acts irresponsibly, and cheats his parents with his lies. He brings a young man called Dukky for his sister Elsie, but he also cheats her and goes back to France. It is at the same time that Sasi, who ruins his own life by overdrinking, returns to Mayyazhi. Maggie, who had ignored him altogether once, repents for what she had done. Elsie, who gives birth to Dukky's daughter, at last becomes a prostitute. Sasi becomes a magician, and following the path of Alphonsacchan, converts stones into toffees for children. Thus the novelist draws our attention to the mischiefs of God on the natives of Mayyazhi, who had always been protected by Adi Billava.

From the point of view of language and technique, the novelist does not go to use any complex mechanism. Though the narration continues till the end in the consciousness of the unknown narrator, in the middle of the novel the journalist Kunjikannan steps into Mayyazhi for collecting various pieces of information about it. At the end also, the same Kunjikannan, after several decades, appears again at Mayyazhi with his educated wife Kalyani, and tells her about the changes that have occurred in the village.

The postcolonial attitude of resistance in the novel runs like an undercurrent throughout, suggesting the bitter truth that the colonial rule was responsible for whatever disaster has taken place in Mayyazhi. Before the coming of the Whites, they were leading a calm life with their innocent faith in Gods and Goddesses of their own. But the Whites taught them the use of money and all the luxuries it brought. The greed for money ruined them altogether. This, in fact, is the intended tone of disapproval, expressly present in the novel.

The Subversive Vision of Life in O.V. Vijayan's *The Legends of Khasak*

O.V. Vijayan is one of the most brilliant and original of the postcolonial Indian authors. He confronts westernization, individualism, homogenization of culture and the nuclear family concepts which are the major postcolonial issues, by giving an entirely subversive vision of them in his first novel *The Legends of Khasak*. Originally written in Malayalam and published in 1968, O.V. Vijayan himself translated it into English in 1994. His employment of techniques like irony, satire, fantasy and magic realism contribute profusely to this subversive vision. It is a vision of life that opposes all kinds of hegemonic oppressions. He attempts to create an alternative view of the society, culture, politics and several other conflicting issues. The way he expresses his protest against the Eurocentric practices like English medicine, English education and chemical contamination of essential things differentiates him from the other Indian writers.

The subversive vision of life presented by Vijayan in *The Legends of Khasak* could be sensed at the superficial level itself. The first reading of the novel gives us the impression that the story line is rather simple, straight and plain. It elaborately gives us the details of the strange experiences of its protagonist Ravi in a remote, backward village called Khasak, a few kilometers away from the township of Palghat in Kerala. Ravi is a young man, with an adventurous spirit in him, always ready to swim against the current. Unlike other young men of the modern times who move towards cities from villages, dreaming of better prospects, Ravi volunteers to choose a small, dark village, far away from the din and bustle of the city. He had been a very intelligent student—a genius—of the Christ College at Tambaram. He had studied there for his B.A. Honours in Astrophysics. Through his active participation in seminars and conferences at college, presenting brilliant papers, he had created a star image of himself. Padma, the daughter of one of his professors was deeply in love with him. One of the visiting professors from the Princeton University in America was greatly impressed by his paper and had invited him to his University to pursue his higher studies on the same subject. But circumstances turn Ravi to be a recluse, letting off all these golden opportunities.

Ravi is a very sensitive man right from the very beginning of his life. He had a loving father and mother. When he was a small boy, his mother used to tell him beautiful stories of Gods and angels dwelling in the sky above. His memories of childhood always began with noon-tide when he sat alone on the veranda of their house on the hilltop:

> His most cherished memory was of the sky-watch, a pastime in which his mother joined him, though not often, as she was big with child. She told him stories of the Devas. These dwellers of the sky drank the milk of the Kalpaka fruit, their elixir of immortality, and flung the empty husks down to the earth. If you gazed on the sky long enough, you saw the husks as transparent apparitions. The sky at noon was full of them. (4)

Ravi's mother had died in childbirth. His father had to marry again. His *Chittamma* (stepmother) was very pretty. After her arrival, Ravi felt alone, having lost the pleasure of his mother's story sessions. He grew up like Cinderella, undergoing a period of orphanhood. He then went to the college at Tambaram and reached the final year of his studies for B.A. Honours. It was then that a shocking incident took place in his life. His father fell seriously ill and was bedridden due to paralysis attack. One day, circumstances led Ravi to share his *Chittamma*'s bed and do the sinful act against his own father. It struck him with an unbearable blow from which he could never come out. He felt that he could never forgive himself. He did not write for the final examination. He gave up his studies, left home without telling anybody and began to wander aimlessly, always thinking and worrying about the meaning of life. He went to Kaasi, he went to Prayag and several other places, and at last took resort in Swami Bodhanand's *asram*. But there also he did not get any peace of mind. The artificiality and hypocrisy of life and the voluptuousness of the *swaminis* at the ashram disgusted him. It was then that he came to learn about the post of a primary school teacher at Khasak to teach the children of the village. After he spends almost a year there, at the end, once again Padma meets him and makes the proposal of marrying him and settling in Princeton with him. But Ravi rejects her, without giving any reason. Perhaps he finds the present system of education and the institution of marriage and family quite meaningless. He comes back to the school only to learn that the District Board has been displeased with him because of an anonymous letter from Khasak, complaining about his misconduct. Of course, Ravi's close friends at Khasak assure him of their full support, and request him to continue there. But Ravi decides to leave the village and continues his journey to the unknown.

This is the outline of the story of *The Legends of Khasak*. However, the novel as a whole is far more than that. Its major part comprises the description of the life at Khasak, its legends, its people, its joys and sorrows, and Ravi's rapt involvement in it. The life at Khasak is an experiment for him. It tells him what the true meaning of life is. It helps him see the different faces of the Ultimate Truth. Though it is an entirely different kind of life, where he had to forego even the basic facilities and comforts of life, he does not get dissuaded. He loves his life and sincerely serves the people there. With his liberal views about true education, he freely mingles with the children and becomes their favourite. He understands the men and women who come to his contact and helps them wherever possible. He develops love, concern and sympathy for the poor and the miserable. Very often, his sense of guilt keeps pricking him, and he decides to atone for it by living for others and loving them.

Ravi's life in Khasak amidst nature—the mysterious *Chetali* hills and valleys—gives him peace and content. He would have continued to live there, had there been no intrusion from the Department of Education. In the novel, the reader is repeatedly reminded of the spiritual journey of the protagonist. The Karma theory has been mentioned again and again, conveying us the message that one has to suffer for the sins he commits in his life—either in this birth itself or the next. One has to carry the burden of his sins on his shoulder till he is redeemed of it. Ravi tries to fulfil this by living the rest of his life at Bodhanand's asram, but fails. It is in his life at Khasak that he puts a step ahead by becoming a child of nature. As we may observe, his is a journey away from civilization to a primitive world. (Here we are reminded of Arun Joshi's novel *The Strange Case of Billy Biswas*) He accepts the uncivilized people of Khasak as his friends. He lives like them—drinking the naturally made toddy and palm wine, believing in their legends, believing in sorcery and witchcraft, accepting quack medicine, enjoying free sex with women whenever he gets an opportunity and so on. He stands neutral with regard to any of the village politics, which, in fact, is roused by the intrusion of the outside world. Though he himself had been brought up in the outside world, which was gradually getting filled up with Communistic principles, Ravi does not develop any faith in it. He knows that there is hypocrisy even among the so-called Communists. That is why he mocks and criticizes their attitude. Life in the folds of nature is the only remedy that he finds. The hidden mysteries of nature always throw a challenge at him, and, trying to bring them out, he continues his spiritual journey.

The Legends of Khasak: Reality through Magic Realism

Magic Realism is a technique used in prose fiction where the writers weave, in an ever-shifting pattern, a sharply etched realism in representing ordinary events and details together with fantastic and dream-like elements, as well as with materials derived from myths and fairy tales. It is a genre where magic elements are a natural part in an otherwise mundane, realistic environment. The fabulous and fantastic elements here are included in the narrative which normally maintains the reliable tone of objective, realistic report designating a tendency of the modern novel to reach beyond the confines of realism and draw upon the energies of fable, folktale and myth, maintaining a strong contemporary social relevance.

The novel *The Legends of Khasak* is replete with the legends prevalent in Khasak, interspersed with fantasies, day-dreams, folktales, sorcery—all these with intermittent references to reality. The effect of this weird world is intensified by the presence of tall trees of Chetali forests, Chetali hills and valleys hung with the ever moving clouds overhead. Ravi's spirit is exalted the moment he steps into the village on seeing the beautiful sight. The first legend that we hear about Khasak is that of Syed Mian Sheik:

> Long long ago in times unknown to man, there came riding into their palmgrove a cavalcade of a thousand and one horses. The riders were the Badrins, warriors blessed by the prophet, and at the head of the column rode the holiest of them all—Sayed mian Sheik (10)

There were 12 mosques in ruins in Khasak, which made a desolate ring round the village. The infinite time of Khasak lay stagnant in them. The legend had it that the pagan deities sought to rebuild the oldest mosque among them. But the deities had sworn that they would do the work of rebuilding it only in the dark, only before daybreak. However the demon spirits who wanted to misguide the deities, turned themselves into roosters and crowed when it was still night. On hearing it, the deities would run away, leaving the building work incomplete. Thus a curse lay on the oldest mosque, and it was left in complete ruins forever. The last mosque among them, the 12th one, was called the Mosque of the King. It was the most recent of the ruins. It overlooked the Araby Tank, which was a pond of crystal water. The people believed that the *Kabandhas*—the dismembered beings in ancient wars came there to wash their unhealed wounds. All these 12 mosques were not used by the Muslims of Khasak for their regular prayers. They built a 13th mosque for the purpose, in which Allah Pitcha Mullah led the prayers.

Ravi had a great zeal to learn more about the myths and legends of Khasak. When he opened the school register, he was baffled to see the names of Caliphs and queens, indigent dynasties which had strayed out of desert sanctuaries and were marooned in Khasak. He kept one hour reserved for telling myths. One day when the children asked him to tell a story, a girl called Kunhamina requested him to tell a *story without dying*. She sang the ballad of Khasak for him, its heroic periods, its torrential winds and its banyan trees. There was no dying there, but only the slow and mysterious transit.

Ravi tells his school children stories based on scientific truths and firmly rooted on reality. After *Onam* vacation, while reopening the school, Ravi saw that the classroom was hung with cobwebs all over. Taking the help of his pupils, he began to remove them. One of the boys asked him what the size of the really big spiders was. Ravi pointed to the dome of the mosque and said that the big spiders were as big as the domes. Outside in the forests of rain, they were born to power and splendor, like the kings of old they revelled in the hunt. And in the teeming nights of fear they rose like the stars of the nether dark: "Ravi told the children the story of the spiders, how after they made love the female ate up her mate. The children could not believe that such bloody dynasties ruled over Khassak's peaceful grass and fern. Then Karuvu stood up and said the male spider was paying for his sins in an earlier birth. The children knew it was Karma, the class was now unusually quiet." (59)

Similarly, there is the story of lizards told by Ravi to children carrying us to a world of fantasy. Chand Umma, the woman who came to cook for Ravi in his kitchen, told him about the death of her husband, along with the legend of the tamarind tree that stood on the edge of the burial ground. The story of Goddess Nallamma, who brings small pox, the story of the power of Kuttadan the oracle, the story of sorcery and witchcraft, Ravi and several other people suffering from small pox which is shown as the wrath of Goddess Nallamma—all these add to the effect of magic realism in the novel.

Tradition versus Modernity in ***Legends of Khassak***

In the traditional world of Khasak, the Muslims and the Hindus lived together in perfect harmony. Misunderstandings and conspiracies begin with the establishing of English schools in the village. In the beginning, it was *Kelan*, the low caste man, who started a school. Till then there was only a *Madrasa* in the village, where Allah Pitcha, the Mullah used to teach religious lessons. In the old system, the beliefs and customs adopted by both the Muslims and the Hindus were the same. All of them believed in the existence of the spirit of Sayed Miyan Sheik, protecting the people of Khasak, and all of them believed in the power of Nallamma, the Goddess of smallpox. They celebrated their Ancestors' Day (séances) on the same day together.

The Mullahs of Khasak were a line of foundlings, all adopted in unusual circumstances. That is why when Allah Pitcha finds the little boy Nijam Ali, he brings him home and decides to make him his successor. However, Nizam Ali turns against Mullah when he grows old. He does not follow the religious principles, and does not agree to tonsure his head or wear a cap. He leaves home, goes to the nearby Koomankavu and works in a beedi factory there. After taking lessons from the people of Palghat about Communism, Nizam Ali rouses the workers of the factory against its master, who had made a lot of money from it. But, for his communistic activities, he was imprisoned, along with the factory owner. However, very cleverly, he escapes from the jail, by convincing the jail authorities that the spirit of Sayed Mian Sheik has come in his dream and has told him to involve himself in social service. That is how he comes back to Khasak after seven years, proclaiming himself to be the *Kazi* of Sayed Miyan Sheik. With the entry of the *Kazi* at Khasak, we see a lot of change in the social life of the village. Allah Pitcha, who is the representative of tradition, feels hurt by the revolutionary attitude of Nizam Ali. The old man is neglected and pushed to a corner.

Sivaraman Nair also represents the old order. He is a landlord. When the District Board sends the proposal of opening a school in the village, Nair offers to assist it by giving his Seedling House free of cost, for the purpose of conducting the classes. When Ravi comes to Khasak, Sivaraman Nair makes arrangement for his stay in the same Seedling House. His nephew Madhavan Nair, who has liberal views against his uncle's orthodoxy, becomes Ravi's friend.

There is some kind of similarity between Ravi and Madhavan Nair. In spite of having a good amount of landed property and money, Madhavan Nair does not go to city and receive education. He stays in Khasak itself as a tailor, incurring his uncle's displeasure. Madhavan Nair supports the school by bringing more children and adding them to the strength of the school. Nizam Ali also extends his helping hand. Shivaraman Nair, who is traditional, withdraws from school when he realizes that Ravi is moving along a new line.

Ravi admits all kinds of children to the school. He does not discriminate between the poor and the rich, the able and the disable, backward and forward, young and old. Even the 20 year old dwarf and mentally retarded Appukili also sits in his class. With tremendous patience Ravi handles them in the class. He does not follow the formal system of text-based teaching. He satisfies their doubts and curiosities by telling them stories. He takes practical classes with live examples. He allows them to copy down things in the examination. He takes them to picnic to the hills and valleys of Chetali. He strongly believes that children can have their true education amidst nature.

We cannot say that the novel puts tradition against modernity. Neither can we say that it rejects modernity in order to move towards a primitive culture. It is not as simple as that. It rather redefines modernity, with an overtone that it would be better to adopt principles which bring us close to nature and take us away from the artificial, hypocritical and the so-called civilized life.

The Fictional Writings of Karanth and Thakazhi from a Feminist Perspective: My Doctoral Thesis

We live in a world of differences and discriminations. Gender discrimination is a glaring one among them. Almost all societies in this world are patriarchal and male-dominated. This is reflected in literature too. In a male-centered world, all literatures have been written and assessed from the male perspective. But when the voice of feminism was raised against the discrimination made against women and when feminism became a movement in the western world, there was a shift in the entire scenario. Then onwards both life and literature were studied from a woman's perspective, in an attempt to throw light on the injustice done to women. Consequently, all the ancient as well as modern literature was studied from a feminist perspective.

The struggle of woman for equality with man has assumed different forms and has yielded mixed results. All feminists—male and female—consider that the ultimate emancipation of humanity is possible only through the emancipation of women. Though there are different feminist organizations and attitudes, only the socialist feminist perspective addresses the issue of gender scientifically. They want to sensitize man and woman about gender status and want collective efforts for the empowerment of women. For women to be free, the deliberate building up of self-confidence, self-understanding, self-respect and the boldness to stand up for the weak in society is essential. The sharing of problems, ideas, information, and the conduct of discussions, debates and collective learning programs can help a woman, move forward to greater freedom and equality. Only an empowered woman, with a developed personality and a realization of the full potential of her identity as woman can be intellectually free. For this a feminist attitude should be developed both in man and woman. And, a very good foundation to this has been laid by the Kannada writer Shivaram Karanth and the Malayalam writer Thakazhi Sivasankara Pillai in many of their novels.

Feminism, mistaken by many, never grudges men. It is nothing but another face of humanism. It fights for women's equal rights, opportunities and status in the society. Not only women, but men also can be the exponents of feminism, provided they have a humane mind to see and understand the truth. Continents may be different. Countries may be different. Cultures may be different. But the cause is the same. It is really amazing to observe that both Karanth and Thakazhi have upheld the same values quite long before feminism became a movement in the world.

I started my investigation on the hypothesis that there are strong feminist concerns in the fictional writings of Shivaram Karanth and Thakazhi Sivasankara Pillai. This made me undertake a comparative study of the two from a feminist perspective. It was with a purpose of throwing light on the feminist concern in the fictional writings of Karanth and Thakazhi and thereby contribute to the feminist criticism.

After writing a preface and giving a brief introduction with a passing reference to the importance of comparative literature in the Indian context, and women in the early Indian novels, in the first chapter, I have discussed the theory of feminism and the details of the feminist movement as it took place in the west. However, I had to disagree to a certain extent with some of the views of the western feminists. As Karanth and Thakazhi seemed to have their own independent views on women's liberation, women's status, women's rights and opportunities in the society, I found it necessary to deviate a little from the western views and develop a theory of Indian feminism, attuning with the theories propounded by the Indian feminists like Vrinda Nabar, Gayatri Spivak, Madhukeeshwar and others. Besides, I studied the status of women in the Indian society right from the ancient *Vedic Age* down to the present times, which might have influenced the thinking of the two authors. I observed that in the *Vedic* society women enjoyed equal rights and opportunities with men and they were not ill-treated or exploited on the basis of their gender. But their position began to deteriorate during the *Smriti Age*, after *Manusmriti* became popular in India.

I started building up an Indian feminism with references to the protests against gender discrimination, shown by different men and women throughout Indian history, right from the *Vedic Age* till the present times. Keeping in view the long-standing tradition, culture and heritage of India I referred to a number of male and female feminists in its history, who have thought and spoken about gender discrimination. I took instances from *Vachana* literature in Karnataka, *Bhakti* poetry all over the country, and the Reformist movement. I have quoted passages from Rigveda, Upanishads, the views of Akkamahadevi and other Sarana Poets, *Bhakti* poets, reformists like Dayananda Saraswati, Ambedkar and others to support my stand.

The *Vedic* Society, as it is elaborated in Rigveda and Upanishads, was amazingly liberal about women, their social and sexual freedom. The changes which took place later may be because of *Manusmriti*, or may be because of the invasion of other religious groups. Karanth and Thakazhi's fictional writings give umpteen examples to expose the absurdities of the male superiority theory, and they uphold the strength of women. They had written these novels long before feminism became a movement in the world. But quite surprisingly, most of the ideas propounded by the western feminists have already come out from these writers in one way or other. Both Karanth and Thakazhi do not agree with the traditional social norms which not only deny rights and opportunities to women, but consider them inferior to men. They deliberately break the myths constructed against women just to generate a general contempt towards them. Through this kind of deconstruction, they seem to proclaim that unless the society gets rid of these constructs, mankind will never live in a happy society. Even the voice of eco-feminism, which is an offshoot of feminism, could be heard in the novels of Karanth and Thakazhi.

Difference from western feminism is obviously seen in the novels of Thakazhi and Karanth in their attitude towards marriage and family life. The basic concept of family life in India is different from that of the west. The sentimental attachment, seeking of mutual co-operation is such that a break between the two would shatter their whole life into pieces. The institution of marriage has been given a kind of religious significance in the Indian cultural and social life. Hence, men and women here are constantly taught to learn tolerance, and develop a feeling of understanding and a sense of attachment. Continuing the progeny is a social obligation which they should take very seriously. The western culture is individual-oriented, whereas the Indian culture is community-oriented. If a marriage is broken, or if a person remains unmarried, it does not become an issue in the western society. But it is not so in India. That *my marriage should be a success* is a feeling deep-rooted in the Indian psyche. Karanth and Thakazhi have dwelt on the Indian culture in their novels, and when they speak against gender discrimination, they never forget to protect the well-being of the family. However, they never protect the family at the expense of the woman suffering as the subaltern. What they say is that, as far as possible, family should be protected by either of the partners, but if it is beyond repair, parting is unobjectionable.

Karanth's novels like *Nambidavara Naaka Naraka*, *Dharmarayana Samsara* and *Sarasammana Samadhi* give the example of such rebellious women who leave their husbands if they are incorrigible. The societal norms, which put so much emphasis on the chastity of woman, are denounced by Karanth and Thakazhi in *Chomana Dudi* and *Chemmeen.* The system of prostitution which was, in fact, was institutionalized by men to satisfy their sexual urge, becomes so cruel that the same men look at them with contempt and hatred and ostracize them. The hypocrisy, treachery and selfishness of men who extract sexual pleasure from the prostitutes are shown in the novels like Thakazhi's *Patita Pankajam*, *Tyagathinu Prathiphalam* and Karanth's *Kanyabali and Maimanagala Suliyalli* where they highlight the virtuous qualities found in the prostitutes. They break the myth that the prostitutes are immoral and advocate the abolition of the system suggestively.

There are premarital and extramarital relationships, and widow marriages in the novels of Thakazhi and Karanth described as sensible and untainted. They do not find fault with those women, instead they express their admiration for them as they have taken a very sensible step in the given situation. They also show how women do not have sexual freedom and how their sexuality is kept under men's control. The myth against female body that it is a seat of sin is strongly attacked by Mookajji of Karanth's *Mookajjiya Kanasugalu.* Mookajji says that no modern human should consider the body, whether a man or a woman, as unholy or its upkeep repugnant. The intellectual freedom of the Indian male and the female is possible only when they bury the dead and sustain the living in Indian philosophy. This is obviously seen in Mookajji. Through this they not only express their concern for women and also oppose the cruelty of men.

Another myth is that women exploit women. The western feminism answers it by proposing *sisterhood* as an antidote. But Karanth and Thakazhi had already broken that myth in many of their novels. We find the bond of true affection between mother-in-law and daughter-in-law, wives of the same husband, women of the neighbourhood and such others. In one of his novels called *Dharmaneethio*, *Alla Jeevitham*, two women love each other so much that they look like lesbians, and they decide that they will not get married. Similar attachment between women could be seen Karanth's *Battada Tore* also. Another myth is the belief that son continues the name of the family, and he protects the family honour. There are many sons in the novels of Karanth who are irresponsible and useless. Instead of sons, daughters and daughters-in-law work hard to protect the family. Another myth is the prejudice against prostitutes. The society believes that the prostitutes are immoral, insensitive, unfeeling and commercial minded. But Karanth's *Maimanagala Suliyalli* and Thakazhi's *Patita Pankajam* prove that it is wrong.

Sociologists and historians tell us that as a social institution, family came into existence only after the evolution of private property and class division. As a result of its long existence, the institution of family has got so deeply entrenched into our socio-psychic system that it appears to be natural and immutable. Different forms of family structures have existed in different areas and at different times. Feudal values are still strong; family has a stronger structure than it has in the capitalist west. As it is women suffer in the family, from the oppressive atmosphere of male domination prevalent there. Traditionally, there is no democracy in the family. The husband is the dictator and the wife is the subject. The woman is confined to the kitchen. Conventionally woman is considered weak. She should be taken care of by the male at all stages of her life. Just like a dog that has begun to love its chain, the woman gets accustomed to her condition. She believes that it is the duty of man to look after her, to protect her, to idolize her. She lacks self-knowledge, and she loses all sense of reality. She begins to think of herself as an adjunct to her husband as his other properties. There is, of course, artificiality in our family structure. There is much hypocrisy and mental tension. This affects the happiness of all the members of the family.

By showing this bitter reality Karanth's *Marali mannige*, *Sarasammana Samadhi* and Thakazhi's *Chemmeen* have suggested that a reconsideration of the family structure based on equality of rights and treatment is necessary.

Critics say that Karanth and Thakazhi, in spite of all their progressive thinking about the marginalization of women, are supporting feudal values by emphasizing on marriage and family. And they also suggest that a reconsideration of the values of family along socialistic lines, where there is a shift in the concept of mother and motherhood is inevitable. But Karanth and Thakazhi have the healthier views because if the family is broken with only mother living with her children, man will be left alone. He will become miserable, without the feeling of any security in life. The purpose of feminism is definitely not isolating men. It never grudges men. Man and woman should live together with mutual understanding of each other. Maybe for this, man has to sacrifice a lot. This kind of a concept of compromise is the life blood of Indian culture. It cannot be denied that happiness of the society is greater than the happiness of the individual. And this has to be achieved by overcoming one's ego.

I have taken only those novels of Karanth and Thakazhi which I found significant from the feminist perspective. I have not considered whether they have been acclaimed as the best works of the authors. That is why, the novels which they have written in the early stage of their career, which have been put aside as immature by the mainstream critics, have also been considered here.

Some of the feminist theories of the west could be applied to Indian feminism too. Without thinking that one day the same views will be put forth by feminists, Karanth and Thakazhi have thrown light on them in their novels. But the difference comes only in man-woman relationship, marriage and motherhood. The radical feminist theory that the institution of marriage should be abolished, or that women should be free from pregnancy and motherhood, are quite unacceptable or impracticable for a man or a woman who are brought up in Indian culture, where people think that life is worth living only if we develop and cultivate a healthy and positive attitude to life by selflessly contributing something to the society, thereby sustaining life and continuing the progeny.

In my comparative study, I have found not only similarities, but some differences too in the fictional writings of Karanth and Thakazhi. But these differences are purely cultural, and not ideological. Karanth deals with upper caste people like Brahmins and Konkanis (*Chomana Dudi* and *Kuduyara Koosu* are exceptions), whereas Thakazhi's novels depict the life of the poor, uneducated, downtrodden and working class people. *Sambandham*, the loose bond of marriage, which though gave sexual freedom to women, had the disadvantage of insecurity. Such relationships we do not find in Karanth's novels. We find maturity of thinking and rationalism among Karanth's women, and uneducated and ordinary women in Thakazhi. But all the same, they exhibit extraordinary courage, confidence and shrewdness in asserting their rights over their husbands and take active part in the family affairs. But for this difference, Karanth and Thakazhi have shown themselves to be very much similar in their revolutionary thinking about a reformed society, without any prejudice or discrimination against women. Though they have not applied advanced theories of feminism, the seeds of feminism that lay a very strong foundation to what was done by the others later in the field, could be seen in their novels. Thus I can say with full confidence that the hypothesis with which I started my investigation has been realized to the maximum extent.

Jesus, I am not a Christian
An Anthology of Thought-Provoking Essays

Dr. K.P. Krishnankutty's *Jesus, I am not a Christian* is a compilation of brainstorming articles on various socially, culturally and politically relevant burning issues. It contains five lectures given by the author on different occasions, and six thought provoking essays on education, knowledge and the place of English in India today.

The book opens with a very interesting and hair-raising article on Jesus and Christianity. At a time when more than three-fourth of the world population is head-over-heels in love with their fond belief in religion and God, the author here is questioning the epistemological relevance and social validity of such beliefs. He says that, though the majority of the Christian priests have dedicated themselves to the service of the poor in diverse ways, priesthood is inherently fascistic as there is an element of one individual privileging upon another. When every human being is born of a natural sexual relationship of his/her parents, and invariably undergoes the same human experiences, why does religion provide the priest spiritual superiority over the laity, forcing them to follow and obey him meekly? Raising this question, the article makes the reader introspect. Speaking about communal harmony, he says that Jesus taught his followers to love their neighbours. But in the world today, people are blind in this regard. They do not love their neighbours, if they belong to any 'other' religion. This is not what Jesus really intended. He said that your neighbour's religion should not block you from loving him. The author says that Jesus was a truly great political revolutionary. He was born in Jerusalem when the situation there demanded someone to lead the Jews out of Roman oppression into the safety of freedom. But the orthodoxy did not read Jesus in this light, and did not preach the political message of Christianity, but simply shrouded him in mysteries.

'I am also a scientist' is an article in which the author says that those who academically pursue the study of science as a subject need not be the real scientists. It is the method of investigation of the human mind that makes one a scientist. Seen from this perspective, the ordinary farmer, working in a field is not different from the specialist scientist in the laboratory, but for his systematic approach and appropriate methodology.

Openly declaring 'I do not know Mathematics,' the author says that the intricacies of Mathematics have made it an unpopular subject. The public attribute the mathematical talent of a person to some divine gift. The author says that this is an idealistic oversimplification. Since every genius is the product of an evolving history, it is their duty to preserve their knowledge for cultural sustenance and survival. Hence the social psyche should be permeated with more of Mathematics and the general awareness of Mathematics should be created in our society through more popular literature on it.

There is a hint against the hypocrisy of the advocates of globalization, who are idealizing it as humanity's great effort to merge into one global family. 'This one world concept is nothing but a euphemism for aggressive capitalism' says the author in an article of the same title. The need for the interdisciplinary research for the purpose of achieving academic integration in college campuses is emphasized in 'Towards a Philosophy of Interdisciplinary Research.' A person's eligibility for this depends on his/her sincerity of commitment to the social relevance of knowledge, which has a political function too.

The second part of the book consists of the author's thoughts on the various facets of the present education system. In the essay 'Education and Value Concepts,' he says that the value consciousness should be a strong hatred for the exploitation of man by man—at the economic, social, political as well as cultural level. Real education should be able to create a social atmosphere that is saturated with friendship and fraternity. Instead of classroom learning, group learning will help cultivate a readiness to share and sacrifice. The system should be made free from ranks and distinctions. Differentiating between knowledge and belief, the author perceives that belief is subjective, but knowledge is objective. If knowledge is to gain total supremacy in an individual's personal and social life, the dominance of subjective conviction over emotional life should be undermined systematically. Whether it is religion or politics, belief is a kind of slavery, and it hinders our knowledge of life and universe.

'A Paradigm Shift in Education' stresses the need of a revolution in the field of education, following the pattern designed by Kerala Sastra Saahitya Parishat. A number of social reformers have already advocated universal education i.e. education for the children of all castes. Immediately after Independence, the first Communist government in Kerala had consistently struggled for the same. But the subsequent governments diluted it. However, the K.S.S.P. once again took it up and carried on its agitation for 'learning and governing in the mother tongue' and conducted a 'Science Culture March' too. This article speaks at length about the efforts put in by the K.S.S.P. for doing justice to the downtrodden masses in the field of education.

The last lengthy article is about the place of English in India today, and the colonial and neocolonial experiences with regard to the use of English. In spite of spending more than 65 years in Independent India, Indians' faith in their own language is dwindling, and their fancy for English is killing the creativity of their native language. The author says that just like the freedom fighters of those good old days, the present day youth should take the learning of Anglo-American language as a challenge. At the same time they should try to put their own mother tongue to digital use, as a defence against neocolonial digital media invasions.

All the articles in the book are based on leftist thinking. All the current issues have been analyzed from a purely scientific perspective. All are scholarly and thought provoking essays, and not meant to be read in a lighter way. An ordinary reader may find their language, style, vocabulary, usages and expressions quite difficult to comprehend. A simpler language would have been able to give even the intellectually downtrodden a comfortable reading.

English Translation of Kannada Poetry: *Fruits and Nuts*

Broadly speaking, translation has been considered rather inevitable in the literary world since time immemorial. Whenever communication between two persons is hindered because of the ignorance of each other's language, there arises the need for a translator or an interpreter. Particularly in a multilingual country like India the problem becomes more knotty in the absence of a common language that can be used by all. It is in this context that English comes to our help. After its advent in India through the British, which happened not more than 400 years ago, English has almost been accepted by all as the *lingua franca*. Today people feel confident that any piece of literary work, if it is translated into English from any regional language, it is sure to reach the readers of all other languages. Besides, an English translation has the possibility of taking a writer to the global heights too. Because of this, A Narsimha Bhat who has already brought some of the classic literary works like D.V.G's. much acclaimed and oft-quoted *Kaggas and* Govind Pai's poetic dramas into English stands important before us. Here I am introducing his recently published anthology of beautiful poems translated from Kannada to English under the title *Fruits and Nuts*.

Since the translator himself is the editor of the anthology here, he has given a very meaningful title to it. *Fruits and Nuts* is a very striking title, indicating the literary taste in the selection of poems made by him. The right selection is the primary task of a translator. The question whether a piece of literature is worth the pain of translation or not is left to the discretion of the translator to decide. 'What am I translating and why am I translating' are the two things that the translator has to ponder over before undertaking the task. Narasimha Bhat's *Fruits and Nuts* justifies itself with full confidence by saying that 'I am presenting to you the fully grown-ups and the still growing-ups.' It is written on the cover page too. 'From Panje to Maheshwari.' He has recorded the best known poems of 115 Kannada poets, most of whom are the lions and tigers of Kannada poetry. Panje Mangesh Rao, Govinda Pai, D.V. Gundappa, Maasti, D.R. Bendre, V. Seetharamayya, Sediyapu, Kadengodlu, Kuvempu, Pu. Thi. No., G.P. Rajaratnam, Dinakara Desai, V.K. Gokak, S.V. Parameshwara Bhat, Kayyar, K.S.N. Swamy, Su. Ram. Ekkundi, Gopalakrishna Adiga among the old heads and G.S.S., Kanvi, N.S.L. Bhat, Nisar Ahmed, H.S. Venkatesh Murti, Siddhalingayya, Malati Pattan Shetty, Vaidehi, Sarvamangala and Maheshwari among the renowned poets of the present times find a prominent place in the anthology with the beautiful translation of their oft-quoted poems. The old poets like Panje, Govinda, Pai, & D.V.G. seem to have left an indelible impression in the mind of the translator with some of their unforgettable poems, because he has translated a number of their popular poems.

Translation of poetry is indeed a herculean task. Retaining the tone, expression, rhymes, alliteration, assonance, music, figures of speeches and other poetic qualities of the original is not that simple. Particularly to find equivalents in an alien language like English needs a lot of knowledge, efficiency and scholarship. Besides, Poetry itself is a tricky genre. More than expressing things openly, it takes pleasure in hiding. Unless the translator is able to elicit the implicated meaning between the lines, he/she cannot render it successfully, in the target language. It is a very tedious exercise. Thus an effective translation of poetry is a challenge to a translator. Narasimha Bhat has won this challenge in his *Fruits and Nuts*. That too, in a context when translators from our regional languages into English are very rare to be found, and when it is the dire need of the times, Mr. Bhat, who has already rendered translations of very important Kannada works into English, should be rightfully recognized for his selfless service.

A Brilliant Translation of the Great Kannada Poet D.V.G.'s *Thus Sang Marula Muniya*

A. Narasimha Bhat's translation of the much acclaimed Kannada poet D.V.G.'s *Marula Munia's verses*, as the title itself says in parenthesis, are the revelations of a spiritual speaker. Translation of poetry, since it is a hard task, is undertaken by a very few and when it is based on spiritual thoughts it is indeed a Herculean task to render it successfully. But Narasimha Bhat's translation has come out so effectively that the experience of reading it not only gives us pleasure but enriches our knowledge of the spiritual world.

These are the musings of the poet himself, who assumes the name of Marula Munia, as he had in his earlier collection of Manku Timma's verses. Here *Marula* (Foolish) Munia himself proclaims that he is the younger brother of *Manku* (Dull) Timma. Though the poet proves himself to be an enormous reservoir of serious thoughts about human life in this world, he becomes the very incarnation of humility in calling himself a fool and a dullard. The verses which this collection consists of are on a variety of topics, related to *Parabrahma* the eternal sprit, Siva the indestructible, indissectable and unattached, awareness of the universality of the self, truth, the enlightened person, the God within us, the individual soul and God, futility of hollow talk and dry disputations, God's grace, fulfilment, our subdued ego, joys and sorrows, patience, the superhuman state, limitations of human ability, world machine, cosmic dance, the beauty and terror of the world, freedom and several other things. On the whole, the spirit behind whatever ideals we find in the Hindu scriptures, have found a space for themselves in all these 806+19 pithy verses.

Bhat's translation too has been rendered in such a simple and lucid style that even an outsider who does not know Kannada can very well feel its familiarity, as D.V.G.'s tough-to-understand ideas have been articulated here in easy English. Look at the verse which elaborates real happiness that one may obtain in human love and human relationships:

> Who is poor? One who hasn't tasted his wife's love,
> One who cannot join the children in their play and enjoy.
> One who cannot forget himself in the cool bliss of the moonlit night,
> A poor mind is poverty personified—Marula Muniya.

Talking about human ego and greed for wealth and fame the poet says:

> Search out the ego in you and find out where and how it is.
> The craving for wealth, sensual pleasures and loving relations
> The craving for fame and titles are all egotism
> Masquerading in various guises—Marula Muniya.

Thus the entire collection is rich with beautiful aphoristic verses of a similar vein throughout and the translation too has retained the freshness of its original.